Luke Karamazov

GREAT LAKES BOOKS

Luke Karamazov

by Conrad Hilberry

FOREWORD BY EMANUEL TANAY, M.D.

Wayne State University Press

Detroit, Michigan 1987

Library of Congress Cataloging-in-Publication Data

Hilberry, Conrad.
  Luke Karamazov.

  (Great Lakes books)
  Bibliography: p.
  1. Searl, Ralph Ray.   2. Crime and criminals—
Michigan—Biography.   3. Mass murder—Michigan.
I. Title.   II. Series.
HV6248.S42H54 1987   364.1'523'0924 [B]   86-28218
ISBN 0-8143-1856-8
ISBN 0-8143-1857-6 (pbk.)

for Marion

Contents

Contents

Contents

Foreword

Luke Karamazov is a dramatic case history of a homicidal psychopath, well written and clinically accurate. But it reads like a murder mystery. When the publisher asked me to comment on the book, I was puzzled. Conrad Hilberry is a writer and a teacher of literature; I am a psychiatrist and a clinical researcher on homicide. Did a homicide expert review *The Brothers Karamazov*, I asked myself? However, I found that here the author has used his literary skills not to create reality but to present it.

Life is stranger than fiction. Poetic license is rather limited when compared to real life. A novelist could not create two brothers who became multiple murderers, much less go on to place them in adjoining maximum-security prison cells numbered one and two; a hero's welcome in a correctional institution given to a brutal killer of five innocent human beings would be objectionable; a vicious killer who becomes a loving husband and father would be unbelievable. Yet you find all that and more in *Luke Karamazov*.

In the psychopathic subculture described by Hilberry, seemingly rational people behave in an irrational manner without being mentally ill. Luke exemplifies the importance of the environment-personality fit. Outside prison he is the

11

ultimate misfit. Inside the walls of a maximum-security peni-
tentiary he is a well-adjusted, respected, and creative mem-
ber of the community. Even though he is a murderous psychopath, he is not devoid of heroic features. One cannot
help but admire the indomitable human spirit demonstrated
by his life. The cruelty of his father, the ineptness of his
mother, and even his own self-destructiveness cannot de-
stroy the vitality of his mind.

The capacity to rationalize, to explain away, to blame
others, and to see oneself as a victim of circumstances is the
essence of the psychopath. Luke fully demonstrates these
qualities. A psychopath has little, if any, conscience and little, if any, control over his impulses. He argues that he is not
responsible because he merely did what he had to do, which
is his way of telling the world that his murderousness is part
of his being and has to be externally controlled.

The variability of the human mind exceeds by far the
variability of the human body. The relative uniformity of the
human physical appearance has created the expectation that
the human personality follows the same general pattern, and
our political and religious traditions reinforce that notion.
This book should help the reader to recognize that we may
all be equal in the eyes of the law or in the teachings of our
religions, but that we differ immensely in our mental
functioning.

Though this book is not the product of the author's
creative imagination, its form is. This is a case history, but it
is also a literary work. Its subject and manner of presentation
will satisfy those who read for entertainment alone. To them
I say: if you liked *In Cold Blood,* you will love *Luke Karamazov.*
Many readers beginning the book may conclude, as I did,
either that this is fiction masquerading as case history or that
Dr. Hilberry was a forensic psychiatrist in his previous life,
for he knows a psychopath when he sees one. Not since
Hervey Cleckley's *Mask of Sanity* has anyone portrayed a
psychopathic personality with such clarity. Students of
human behavior will find the book an interesting study of a

pathological family which produced two brothers who are multiple murderers. Other professionals, like judges, probation officers, school teachers, and others who deal with psychopaths, will find it required reading.

Emanuel Tanay, M.D.

Acknowledgments

I wish to thank Luke Karamazov, Tommy Searl, and Julie Karamazov for their willingness to discuss their lives with me; their talk gives the book its vividness and flavor, its immediacy. Thanks also to Alfred Gemrich, who first proposed this project, and to Defense Attorney Eugene Field and Kalamazoo County Prosecutor James Gregart, who encouraged the study and made court transcripts and other information available to me. Prison officials in Ionia and Marquette were unfailingly courteous, candid, and helpful. And Blaine Lam graciously supplied me information he had collected when he covered this story for the Kalamazoo *Gazette*.

More personally, I would like to thank my colleagues Robert Grossman of the Psychology Department and Richard Means of the Sociology Department at Kalamazoo College for discussing the Searl brothers with me and helping me clarify my views of them. Long-time friends Laurence Barrett and Edward Galligan, both English professors, and Richard Kinney, Acting Director of the Wayne State University Press, all read earlier versions of the manuscript and made sound and insightful suggestions; the book is greatly improved by their help. I am grateful for the interest and support of Provost Warren Board and other friends at Kalamazoo College and, as always, for the help of my wife Marion.

Author's Note

The people and events here are real; I have taken pains to check the facts and present them accurately. But, except for a few public figures in Kalamazoo (judges, attorneys, a psychologist, and a newspaper editor), I have used fictitious names in order to protect the privacy of the actors in the story and their families.

1.

Luke Karamazov

I came in with the attitude, OK, I'm guilty, what the hell, I'm in the right place. I suppose I did like it too. I'd be lying if I said I didn't like it. When I first came in, you know, "That's him! That's the one, right there!" At that time, all the lifers stuck together, and no matter what joint I walked into there was always somebody saying, you know, "You need anything? Money? What do you need?" Other lifers saying, "I got a picture that would look cool on that wall there." They decked the joint out so when I first came in it was almost like coming home. And it's a pretty heady experience for a young kid to evoke so much terror in people, you know?

The kid enjoying the heady experience was Ralph Ray Searl, who confessed to killing five men over a period of two and a half months in the spring of 1964. He was tried for only one of the five murders—the shooting of Earl Foote, a school teacher who picked him up, hitch-hiking, on West Main Street in Kalamazoo, Michigan. The case got a great deal of publicity, both before and after Searl was arrested, and dur-

19

ing the trial which was a long one. By the time Searl was finally convicted of first-degree murder and sentenced to life in prison, he was notorious. The lifers at the State House of Correction at Marquette might well take notice of the nine-teen-year-old white man who had pulled a gun on a teacher, told him to drive onto the back roads across U.S. 131 west of town, robbed him of his shoes, his watch, and the three dollars in his wallet, and then forced him into the trunk of his own 1963 Chevrolet.

Later, Searl explained that he had told the teacher to be quiet back there and not cause any trouble. Then as he was driving along the dirt roads wondering what to do next, he heard a thumping in the back of the car. At first, he thought it was just the rough road, but, driving over a smooth stretch, he realized that the thumping was the teacher pounding on the roof of the trunk. Searl was annoyed. He had *told* the man to be quiet. He got out, opened the trunk, tied up Foote with a rope he found in the car, and shot him through the head. Then, with the body in the trunk, he drove south on U.S. 131, stopped at a hamburger stand in Schoolcraft, and ordered a hamburger and a Coke, saving some of the Coke to wash the blood off the car.

That same night, Searl says, he drove south to Elkhart, Indiana, and parked near an all-night gas station to wait until there were no customers. He fell asleep for a few hours, then awoke, robbed the gas station, killed the attendant, and headed back north to Kalamazoo. On the way, as he drove around a curve near Three Rivers, not far over the Michigan state line, he came upon a police road block set up to stop whoever had committed the robbery and murder in Elkhart. Searl coolly drove up to the police car and asked, "What's the trouble, officer?" The policeman waved him through, and he drove on to Kalamazoo in Foote's car, the body still in the trunk. Weeks before, as it turned out, he had killed three other men—two of them gas station attendants and the third a man who had picked him up when he was hitch-hiking in Nevada. Not all of this had been in the newspapers, but much of it had. The prisoners at Marquette had reason to treat Searl, on his arrival, with respect and even awe, emotions he had seldom evoked before.

The corner of West Main Street and Douglas Avenue, where Ralph Searl was hitch-hiking on the night of Foote's murder, is across the street from Kalamazoo College, where I taught then and still teach. I passed that corner every day, on foot or in the car, and I used to pick up hitch-hikers from time to time. When the Kalamazoo *Gazette* was giving front page space to Searl's apprehension and trial, it occurred to me that the dead teacher could just as well have been myself.

After Searl's conviction and imprisonment, Kalamazoo gradually forgot about his murders, a grisly bit of history that slipped further and further back in everybody's mind. But in 1971, Searl's name was back in the paper. Eugene Field, his court-appointed attorney, had appealed the decision on procedural grounds. When Searl was first taken prisoner on June 5, 1964, he confessed to the five murders and, when asked, said he did not want to be represented by counsel at his trial. Later that night, at a special 4:00 A.M. arraignment before Judge Clark Olmsted, he was again offered an attorney; again he refused. But at about 8:00 A.M. the next morning, just before he was to be examined by two psychiatrists from the Kalamazoo State Hospital, Searl said to an assistant prosecuting attorney, "You mentioned something about an attorney. I think maybe I better have one." The Assistant Prosecutor told him that a magistrate would arrive at 9:30 A.M. and a lawyer could be appointed at that time. The psychiatric examination sought by the prosecutor took place as scheduled, before Field was appointed to defend Searl, and the psychiatrists' testimony turned out to be important to the prosecutor's case against Searl. During the trial, Field undertook to persuade the jury that Searl had been insane at the time of the murders, and to refute this claim the prosecution made extensive use of the testimony of the state psychiatrists, based on that early morning examination.

The legal procedural point, then, was that Searl, because he was not allowed to talk with his attorney before the psychiatric interview, was deprived of his right to counsel and, in effect, denied his right not to testify against himself. Field pursued this appeal through the courts and in 1971 won his point before the Michigan Supreme Court, which sent the case back to the Kalamazoo Circuit Court for retrial. The prosecutor appealed the decision of the state Supreme Court to the United States Supreme Court but did not succeed in getting it reversed.

So Searl returned to the county jail and Kalamazoo was forced to acknowledge again the person who may well be the coolest, most matter-of-fact killer in the city's history. But the case did not come to trial a second time. In the intervening seven years, Searl's plea of temporary insanity had become somewhat less plausible than it was in 1964—he had been a tough and aggressive prisoner at Marquette, but not an insane one—so he pled guilty. The details of the plea bargain have never been made public, but apparently he bargained for a couple of concessions: that he be imprisoned in the Michigan Reformatory at Ionia, a maximum security prison primarily for young offenders, instead of one of the larger prisons at Marquette or Jackson; and that he be permitted to change his name to Luke Karamazov.

If that were all, newspaper readers in Kalamazoo would have talked for a while about this murderer who appealed his case all the way to the Supreme Court and then pled guilty; we would have wondered about this man with the curiously literary taste in names; and then we would have forgotten him.

But on March 20, 1972, while Ralph Searl was still awaiting retrial, the Kalamazoo *Gazette* reported that the body of a young woman, Cynthia Kohls, had been found behind the Independent Elevator Company building on Peekstock Street on the outskirts of Kalamazoo. A passerby noticed a year-and-a-half old boy crying, his hands and shoes covered with blood. The child led neighbors around the building to his mother's body. It was later discovered that she had been abducted the previous evening near the discount store where she and the child had been shopping: her car was found in the parking lot. Mother and son were taken to the more isolated spot on Peekstock where the mother was raped and stabbed to death with a knife. At the time, there were no clues as to who the rapist-murderer might be.

Four months later, on July 17, two decomposed bodies were found by motorcyclists in a wooded area north of the Kalamazoo River near Galesburg—perhaps a dozen miles from Kalamazoo. The bodies were those of two nineteen-year-old women, Cornelia Davault and Nancy Harte, who had set out from Chicago on July 5 on their way to Ann Arbor. The bodies were found in the back seat of the blue Opel Kadett that belonged to the parents of one of the women. One woman had a gag in her mouth; the other apparently had been strangled by a nylon rope around her neck. Again, the police had no immediate suspects. On August 5, Jennifer Curran, a nineteen-year-old student at Western Michigan University, went on a shopping errand and never returned.

On September 5, the *Gazette* reported that a twenty-eight-year-old service station attendant and a fifteen-year-old boy had been arrested and charged with the murder of the two Chicago women. The man was Tommy Searl, the older brother of Ralph. Later he was charged with the rape and murder of Cynthia Kohls and of Jennifer Curran. Curran's body was found, in October, near the Kalamazoo River, less than a mile from the place where the bodies of the Chicago women had been discovered. When Tommy was taken into custody, Ralph was also being held in the County Jail, awaiting retrial. They occupied maximum security cells number one and number two.

Unlike Ralph, Tommy did not admit to having committed the murders—he still claims to be innocent. The Prosecutor Donald Burge and Assistant Prosecutor James Gregart undertook to prove him guilty of the murder of all four young women, so that there would be no chance of his being freed because of a procedural error. Off and on for a full year, the paper carried stories of arraignments, preliminary examinations, and two jury trials, one running ten days, the other two weeks. The key witness for the prosecution was Kerry Weiser, Tommy's fifteen-year-old friend who admitted to having committed three of the rape-murders along with Searl. His memory was vivid and the police and prosecutors were thorough. Before the trials ended, everyone in the city must have carried images of women forced to dress and undress, repeated rape in Searl's van, strangulation with nylon cord, and suffocation with a yellow plastic bag. By the end of the year, juries had found Tommy Searl guilty of the murders of Cynthia Kohls and Jennifer Curran, and he had pled no contest to the murder of the two Chicago women. The name *Searl* had been scratched on everyone's memory.

By the fall of 1973, when Tommy was taken away to the State House of Correction at Marquette and Ralph to the Michigan Reformatory at Ionia, revulsion was the prevailing mood. Hayden Bradford, City Editor of the Kalamazoo *Gazette*, told me that the staff had chosen their Searl coverage as the best news story of the year, but he disagreed. He and the reporters had overdone it, he thought; they had conducted the trial in the paper. Looking back over those issues of the *Gazette*, I don't see that he could have given it less space than he did, or more objective coverage—but at the time his distaste overcame the pride he might have felt in a full and accurate job of reporting. Judge Lucien Sweet, who presided over the Curran trial, says he still asks his wife not to keep yellow plastic garbage bags around the kitchen.

Early in 1976, Alfred Gemrich, a Kalamazoo attorney, pointed out to his acquaintances that this case might be unique in the annals of crime—two brothers each convicted separately of serial murders. Someone, he thought, ought to collect some information about them while it could still be found. By this time, revulsion had worn off somewhat, and, prodded by Gemrich's interest, I began to wonder who these men were and how they got that way. I wondered if I could talk with them.

Gemrich introduced me to Eugene Field, the attorney who had defended Ralph Searl and successfully appealed his conviction. Field said he thought Searl (now Luke Karamazov) would be willing to talk with me, and he loaned me the 1,118-page transcript of his trial. In September 1976 I wrote to Karamazov, saying very briefly that I was interested in writing something about him and his family, I didn't know exactly what, and asking whether he would be willing to talk with me. He replied promptly with a typed letter which began:

> Dear Mr. Hilberry:
> Received your letter of September 8. I have given your proposal a good deal of serious thought, regretably the best I can offer at this point is a tentative "I don't know."

He went on to say that he would need to know more about what I had in mind. He noted my willingness to come to Ionia to talk further about it, but there was a problem. He was allowed only five regular visits per month, and he could not consider using those visits for anyone other than his wife. He told me, however, exactly how I should proceed to arrange an "attorney-type" visit that would not count against his quota of five regular visits. The letter concluded:

> In all fairness I feel that I should give you some idea of my feelings in this matter. I assume that you see some type of personal reward for yourself in this task, by the same token I can see some personal benefits for myself also, however I am not particularly interested in any more sensationalist propaganda. If on the other hand you are interested in a in-depth study that might serve to

answer serious questions as to the inner workings of this particular mind I would be only too happy to assist you in this quest.

Thanking you for your interest I am,

Sincerely yours

Luke Karamazov

I accepted his definition of what we were up to and wrote to the prison officials, sending him a carbon of the letter as he said I should. Instead of hearing from the Director of Treatment, to whom I had written, I heard from Karamazov himself. He now addressed me by my first name.

Dear Conrad:

Hello, received your thoughtfully prompt reply, thank you for your consideration.

I have conferred with Glen Langdon and Deputy Warden Jespersen concerning your request for a special visit, and I am happy to say this has been granted and is scheduled to take place Oct. 14th at 2:00 PM. I look forward to our meeting that date.

Glen asked me to inform you of the decision in lieu of writing you himself, so please consider this his reply.

He went on to tell about the arrangements that had been made to assure my admission and to explain what I should do if I had any difficulty getting in: "As always, when one is dealing with a bureaucracy one must be prepared for foul-ups. If it should happen that there is some problem in being allowed in, simply request to speak to Deputy Warden Jespersen or Director of Treatment Glen Langdon and all doors will open promptly." Clearly, the man I was going to visit was not the sullen, inarticulate inmate I had half imagined him to be. He was evidently quick, taking pleasure in the movement of a sentence, and certainly he knew his way around the prison.

Before the visit I received another note, handwritten this time:

Dear Conrad:
   Hello again. Sorry to bother you but I just thought of a slight problem; we have a rule here that Residents (me) are not allowed to carry cigarettes thru the visiting gate, being that I am a life long smoker I find it most uncomfortable to be forced into a situation wherein I can't smoke. Visitors are however allowed to carry cigarettes into the visiting area. If it wouldn't be too much trouble could you kindly purchase a pack of Winston's and bring them Thursday? Also there is a pop machine (25¢) in the area we will meet in, if we are to be meeting for any extended period of time a cold drink might be nice? I will instruct my wife to forward a $2.00 check to you this week to cover these items. Thank You.
                     Most Sincerely Yours
                     Luke

When I set out for the prison, I had a pack of Winstons in my pocket and plenty of quarters. (His wife mailed me the two-dollar check, which I did not cash.) The Michigan Reformatory at Ionia is a large, old prison, walls of white-painted brick with barbed wire at the top and guard towers at the corners. I drove up an angling road toward the prison, parked the car, and hesitated at a guard house beside the walk. A policeman pointed to the prison door. As I approached, four guards came out the door dressed in kelly green jackets, evidently a uniform. They were relaxed, pushing each other and laughing, talking about salmon fishing and how much one of them had paid for a Dodge pickup. They looked like members of a slow-pitch softball team coming out of the showers. Somehow, it didn't seem right.

Inside, I waited in line behind some other visitors, an older woman and a younger one, perhaps the mother and sister of a prisoner. I told the woman behind a wire-mesh screen that I had come to see Luke Karamazov. The name clearly was familiar to her and did not seem strange. She checked my driver's license and told me to put my valuables in a locker across the room and then sit down; they would call me. The waiting room was painted cinderblock with a tile floor; it was furnished with a plastic sofa, some chairs, ash trays, and a pop machine. At one end of the room, inmates lounged behind the counter of a small concession stand, ready to sell cigarettes or candy. Two or three groups talked quietly—wives, children, brothers, or friends. That afternoon they were all black. After twenty minutes or so, a voice over a loudspeaker said, "Karamazov." I went back to the wire cage where the woman marked the back of my hand with invisible ink from a felt-tipped marker. A guard frisked me, took a look at the folder of blank paper I had with me, and motioned to a man in a control booth behind a thick glass door. The door slid open and I walked through, putting my hand under a fluorescent light at the control booth. The invisible ink glowed. Another glass door slid open and I walked into the visiting room.

Before I could wonder what to do next, a young man approached me, shook hands, and introduced himself as Luke Karamazov. He was wearing a light blue leisure suit with a flowered sport shirt turned out over the collar of the suit. His hair was long, well down over his ears; a moustache and a pointed Vandyke beard gave him a faintly Mephistophelian look. He wore dark glasses. I had been somewhat apprehensive. I had never been inside a prison before, never met a murderer. But Luke looked around the room, which had the feeling of a small-town bus station—fiberglass chairs in rows, low formica tables, ashtrays, Coke cans, knots of people here and there, talking—and suggested that we sit at a small table on a slightly raised section of the floor. The difference in height gave us a sense of privacy, as though, looking down on the other groups, we could not be heard or seen. In fact, we did have privacy enough. Noisy as the room was, it would have been hard for anyone to overhear us, and no one tried.

I gave Karamazov the cigarettes and matches, and he got us each a Coke from the machine. I asked about his name. He explained that in the neighborhood where he grew up, on East Main Street in Kalamazoo, everybody talked about those damned Searl kids. In prison he was always called by his last name. He hated it. He shrivelled inside every time he heard "Searl." So he changed it to something that would intrigue everybody—it would give them an impression. Everyone, he said, should be able to choose his own name. Damn what Mom wanted back then.

We spoke for a few minutes about my vaguely conceived writing project. Mainly Karamazov told me about himself, while I wrote as fast as I could. I asked questions from time to time—I knew a good deal about his life from reading the transcript of his trial—but he needed little prompting. He spoke easily and emphatically about the disappointing trip he had made, when he was fifteen, to visit his father in Florida; about Betty Fitzell, the woman, ten years older than himself, whom he had lived with; about his nearly successful suicide attempt before the murders; and about the murders themselves. After talking in detail about the killings, he added, "What strikes me as strange is how I could so calmly kill someone, yet I'm very reluctant to hurt someone. That's what I wonder about my mind: how it handles that transition."

He spoke of his wife Julie, whom he had married in a prison ceremony just seven months earlier. They had gone out together sometimes in high school, and she had admired him at a distance while he was in the army and during the time he was living with Betty Fitzell. When he was convicted of murder, she married his brother Tommy, "more for the name than for the person." After half a dozen years, she divorced Tommy and married Ralph's best friend, Bob

Melos. Later she divorced Melos and married Ralph. Now, he wrote to her nearly every night and wrote often to her four children, whom he thought of as his own. He couldn't do anything now, he said, without thinking how it would affect them. Looking back, it didn't seem to him that he had had a family when he was growing up. Now Julie and her children had supplied one. He had held it in abeyance all this time, his desire for a family.

In Ionia he had taken over a watch repair business from another prisoner who had left. "I taught myself to repair watches—one way or another I learned it." He had some watch works and he wanted to make a watch with a special case as a present for his wife. He wanted to invest a lot of time and emotion in it. At first he couldn't think what material he could use for the case. There isn't much to work with in a prison. He settled on the pink plastic material they use to make dentures. With a razor blade and sandpaper, he formed a heart-shaped case out of the plastic and set the works and a crystal in it. He made a loop so that Julie could wear it around her neck. The face of the watch was a photograph of Luke Karamazov himself. "I'm a genius," he said. "I really am. I'm a genius at improvising."

No one came to interrupt our conversation; I guess we could have talked till suppertime, or beyond. But after a couple of hours I was tired from my high-speed note taking, from trying to get this strange information down correctly, trying to get enough of his words verbatim so that I could reconstruct his style of thought and speech. A tape recorder would make it a lot easier. I asked Karamazov if he thought the prison officials would permit me to bring one. He said they probably would, and he told me what I should say in my letter to the Deputy Warden: I should explain that a tape recorder would make it possible for us to work more efficiently and in that way complete the project with fewer visits to the prison. That would sound like a legitimate reason. It seemed a good reason to me, too, though not the only reason, and I later wrote to the Deputy Warden saying what

Karamazov suggested. The permission was granted, and subsequent interviews with Karamazov, his wife Julie, and his brother Tommy were taped. Interviews with prison officials and others I have recalled from notes.

We made tentative plans for another visit a month later and I left, passing out through the sliding glass doors again and picking up my belongings from the locker. On the way home I had time to wonder what sort of man this was, this devoted husband behind the beard and dark glasses, this inmate who had figured out what would open doors within the prison, this man who admitted liking it there and who talked matter-of-factly about the sense of wonder he felt in seeing how far the blood spurted from the head of a man he had shot. My central impression was one I have not adequately conveyed yet, but one that will become clearer as we go on: the impression of intensity and power. Certainly he was affable and courteous, making the visit much easier than I had imagined it might be. At the same time, he seemed completely in control, saying just what he intended to say, well aware of the impression he was conveying. He might well be a genius at improvising, I thought, and his improvisations probably included management of people as well as shaping hearts from pink plastic. He had been a prisoner for twelve years, yet he was not festering, as I had imagined he would be, under the boredom and humiliation of an overcrowded, maximum security prison. Somehow, he seemed to be running the place.

When he spoke of changing his name, I remembered, he said that in Marquette he had spent long periods of time in solitary confinement, "isolating all the negatives in my mind and expunging them." He had progressed further than anyone he had known in self-improvement and he confessed to being "arrogantly proud." The cold pride was evident, I thought, underneath his thoroughly reasonable conversation and his apparently frank self-revelation. And always there was the feeling of power. If I had been a prisoner in Marquette, I would have feared him.

31

Luke Karamazov

Driving toward Kalamazoo, I wondered about the child-hood of these two brothers, how they had become what they were. But I also wondered about the present life of Luke Karamazov. What negatives had he expunged? How could one reconcile his devotion to his newly acquired family with the casual, remorseless way he spoke of the murder of five men, some of them husbands and fathers. I remembered his exhilaration at entering prison as a sort of hero, a famous killer, and it occurred to me that he might have more power, greater control over his life and his surroundings here in the closed world of the prison than he ever had had as a free man, undistinguished by murder.

2.

Childhood: Father

When I walked through the sliding glass doors a month later, Karamazov met me again and took me, this time, to the Parole Board Room, a small, plain room separated from the visiting room by a wall with large glass windows. It was a perfect place to talk, except that the radiator sometimes clanged like a construction crew. I brought the tape recorder this time, as I did on subsequent visits, and we let it run through the whole conversation. The transcriptions here are edited to eliminate repetitions, false starts, etc. I am aware that in reproducing Karamazov's own account of his life, I permit him to color the events as he chooses. As we will see, part of the interest in his history lies in this very coloring.

This time Karamazov began by asking about my notes taken the month before. Were they disorganized? How do I go about organizing my material? He was afraid I might come out with a stack of scattered observations and have a year's work sorting them out. So he proposed that we go year by year. I agreed and suggested that he start with the earliest memories he could call up.

Really, a relevant memory, one of the first memories, is my brother and I taking father's pistols,

OK? Now he had two pistols. I'm fairly certain
they were both .32's—maybe one was a .22 and
the other a .32. I believe I was pre-school at the
time, probably four, possibly in kindergarten. I
know it had to be in that range because we moved
when I went to first grade. What we did is, we
stole the pistols, went down to the river near the
Kilowatt Lake, they called it. We went down there
and shot at birds. I don't know. To me it seems
extraordinary, as I think back. [I admitted that it
seemed extraordinary to me, too.] The overpower-
ing emotion that comes to mind is the power of this
weapon, you know, the noise and the impact. I can
remember the bullet hitting the sand. They were
swallows, bank swallows we were shooting at. We
were more or less shooting at holes, really. They
were inside and we'd shoot and one'd come flying
out. We weren't actually shooting at birds, more so
at holes, but I can remember the bullet hitting the
dirt, the sandy, loose dirt, and it'd just explode,
you know? I remember the power of it right then.

There were four children in the Searl family: Leslie, the
oldest; Tommy and Ralph, about a year apart; and finally
Sally, four years younger than Ralph. Until the boys were of
school age, the family lived out of town near a dammed-up
section of the Kalamazoo River known as Kilowatt Lake because of the power station at the dam. Though he was still
young when the family moved to town, Ralph remembers
with pleasure the scraggly, semi-rural oak and sumac country near the town of Comstock, where he and Tommy shot at
swallows. It was to these back roads and woods near Kilowatt Lake that Tommy and his accomplice, twenty years
later, took three young women to rape and murder them—
if, in fact, Tommy is guilty as the jury found him to be.

When the children were old enough for school, the family moved to a small house in Kalamazoo. They lived in a

lower middle class section of town, the house facing the steep part of East Main Street, one of the chief thoroughfares in the city. Behind the house were a gravel pit, railroad tracks, a truck yard, and the semi-industrial lots and sheds one finds on the less prosperous side of a city. Ralph and Tommy both remember flying on sleds or bicycles down the East Main hill, stealing rhubarb, getting in rock fights, and walking precariously on the railroad trestle over the river.

In spite of their closeness in age and the days and years they spent together, it seems to Ralph, in retrospect, that there was always a distance between him and Tommy. "I don't remember being attached to anyone, at all. I know Tommy had Leslie, they were inseparable. Sally was too young. Leslie, she always took Tommy's side because he caught most of the hell. I was the youngest boy so naturally I got out of a lot of the trouble. You know, it was his fault because he was the older one. So no one was really attached to me, and I've never got attached to anyone else. I suppose what it boiled down to was I was kind of a loner."

An incident may indicate how deep this detachment went. When the family lived out by Kilowatt Lake, Dennis Searl, the boys' father—a strong man in spite of a withered arm—drove a semi-truck. One day, perhaps drunk, he ran over the family dog with the truck. "The other kids were more terrified, more upset than I was. I remember I looked at the other kids and I thought, how could they be so attached to a dog to cry, you know, or have a tantrum. I remember being in wonder how the other kids could be so attached." As he was saying this, Karamazov was aware, I think, that to me he seemed strangely detached, even now. In our first meeting, I had been struck by the eerie casualness with which he accommodated himself to murder. Perhaps sensing this reaction, he was locating this same detachment in his earliest childhood.

Norma Searl, the mother, seems to have been baffled or overwhelmed by her children. When they were growing up, she worked much of the time at a paper factory in Kalamazoo, choosing the afternoon shift from 3:00 P.M. to 11:00 P.M. so that she was seldom home when the children were there. According to Ralph, his mother, though she tried, was not well equipped mentally or emotionally for the traumas she went through. She was disorganized, not able to deal with the kids. Ralph decided there was no use investing emotion in her. Besides, he blamed her for his ears, which were a constant source of embarrassment to him. They stuck out, making him look, he says, like a taxicab with the back doors open. Once his uncle told him that his ears stuck out because, when he was small, his mother made him wear a flier's cap and she had put it on wrong, folding his ears forward by mistake. He never had any doubt, as a boy, that his ears were her fault.

Beginning with the bank swallows, the motif of power—or, more often, powerlessness—runs through Searl's recollections of his childhood. His father apparently took pleasure in frightening or humiliating the boys. When they were still very young, his father put Ralph behind him on his motorcycle.

> I distinctly remember the big leather seat that just kind of comes up around you. And he took off lickety-split across this briar patch. It was hilly, bumpy, briary ground, you know, logs and everything laying all over. He's got the handlebars to hang onto and I've got nothing. I'm literally being thrown up and down and just terrified. I was preschool at that time too, four or five years old. I know I disliked the old man for doing it. I thought he was, you know, pretty stupid and cruel. That was the first thing I remember him doing *to* me.

Later he remembers his father feeding whiskey to him and his brother, urging them to drink it in one gulp and be a man. He remembers his father catching a snapping turtle and putting it at them, telling them what it would do to them.

Sometimes, when the children did not obey quickly enough, their father became enraged:

> He'd be downstairs and our bedrooms were up-
> stairs. We'd be playing in the bedroom when we
> were supposed to be going to sleep, wrestling or
> whatever. So he'd holler one time from his bed-
> room or wherever he happened to be setting. Nat-
> urally, we wouldn't pay any attention. Then he'd
> holler from the bottom of the stairs. If there was
> one more peep after that, up those stairs he'd
> come. He'd come up there two at a time and you'd
> hear him whipping that belt out. I can distinctly
> remember it whipping through the belt loops. And
> as soon as he hit the top of the stairs, whichever
> one he thought made the noise, here he'd come.
> He wouldn't turn on a light or nothing, he'd just
> start swinging that strap. He almost killed Leslie
> doing that. He hit her on the top of the head with
> the buckle. I can still feel him running up the stairs,
> the weight of him on those stairs.

The children were not the only ones in the household to feel their father's fury. One morning when their mother failed to wake the children, Ralph, then six or seven, went down to her room and found the mirror broken, the dressers emptied on the floor, cheap jewelry scattered all over the room.

> She had a white chenille bedspread, and she was
> laying on the bedspread, and there was blood just
> literally all over. It was red with blood. You know I
> remember it that way, it probably wasn't that bad.
> But there was blood all over the walls and ceiling.
> You know I'm a little kid and I walk in there—
> What's happening Mom, how come you didn't get
> us up?—and, boom, I'm confronted by this. She
> had blond hair and it was just matted with blood.

What he had done is, he had broke her nose and broke both her lips open. I don't know if I went to her or if I just stood and looked. I can't say at this point. But every time I think of it, I just see red, not anger red but blood red.

Karamazov speaks of this scene again later. It impressed him deeply, as well it might. Ernest Becker in *The Denial of Death*, a book I will be coming back to for help in understanding other aspects of Searl's career and personality, argues that the fear of death lurks just beneath the ordinary activities of our lives. Following post-Freudian psychologists, he finds that scenes in which a child discovers menstrual blood are deeply traumatic because they leave no doubt that the mother, on whom the child depends for everything, is herself thoroughly vulnerable. There is no mistaking her physicalness, her mortality. If this is true of ordinary mothers and children, where the blood is normal menstrual flow, how much more intense must the effect be where the blood is shed violently and the mother's helplessness is far more than symbolic.

Dennis Searl's violence, beating members of his family and shattering the house, was a more or less constant threat while he lived there.

We had a piano, a big grand piano. I don't know where we had got it at. It took up almost the whole front room. It was for my sister; they wanted her to play the piano, Mom did. But he came home drunk and destroyed that piano, broke it up in such small pieces that he ended up throwing it all out the door, threw it all out in the yard. He had one arm, was all he used. The other one had been shot through the wrist and had a big crater in it. All he could do with that hand was steady things. He could hardly hold a book of matches in it. His other arm was literally twice the size of the injured one. He injured it when he was twelve years old, a shotgun accident. But he always—I don't know when I

38

started understanding but at some point I came to understand—he had to prove himself to other men. He was constantly fighting, getting drunk and fighting and picking up women to prove that he was a whole man.

This analysis of the father by the son may well be accurate, though it includes no sense of irony, no acknowledgment that anyone else in the family might have used violence to prove his manhood.

Dennis Searl left the family when the boys were nine and ten, his arbitrariness and brutality having given them little sense that their surroundings were comprehensible, to say nothing of controllable. He had shown them no legitimate way to earn approval or self-esteem. If they felt driven to be heroes, as Becker claims all children do, they could not learn from him that a person can earn his heroism through sustained work or genuine invention. The father's heroics took the form of impulsive violence and cruelty.

From Kalamazoo, Dennis Searl went to Florida and married again, married a woman who tried tenaciously for a little stability in *her* life. During their teens, each of the boys hitch-hiked to Florida to find their father, who owned a gas station there. The visits led only to renewed bitterness and separation. A letter from Dennis Searl's second wife somehow made its way into the transcript of Ralph's trial. Tommy had written to ask if he could come to Florida to visit his father. Apparently he had mentioned Ralph's discharge from the army, in the fall of 1963, after he had spent his last ninety days locked up in the stockade:

November 19, 1963

Hi, Tom:

Since Dennis don't want to answer, then I will. Dennis don't want to hear from you or any of you up that way. We have all we can do taking care of our station. When you come down here, you bring us trouble. Dennis and I are getting along just fine now and I am going to keep it that way. If he wanted you down here, he would have wrote you so. He don't even think of you at all. So forget us down here. Can't you see you are not wanted here? So don't push yourself where you are not wanted.

As for your birthday, I wish you a happy one. When Dennis read the letter about Ralph, he said then that he didn't want to hear from you or see you all. So, don't write us anymore. He let me read your letters before he does; that is how much he cares about you. As for your girl friend, he said you could have done better. But I am trying to get Dennis to write you, but if he does it will be because I made him write. Lots of luck.

Though this second Mrs. Searl is not related to Ralph and Tommy, her letter conveys a sense of weariness, of just barely hanging on, that probably characterized Searl's first family as well. And it completes the rejection of the boys by their father.

A psychiatrist from Ann Arbor who testified for the defense in Ralph's trial argued that his murders were symbolic attempts to get back at his father. Three of the men he killed were gas station attendants: his father ran a gas station. Several of his victims were short and dark haired: so was his father. His fury at his father amounted to a temporary madness, transferred to people who reminded him of his father. The jury was not convinced by the argument and, in fact, neither was Searl. Afterwards, he said that the gas stations were most likely convenient places to rob, and he followed through with the murders almost mechanically, eliminating witnesses, playing out the role. He says he did take a technical interest in the killings; he experimented with death, convinced that he would die soon himself. But he doesn't believe that the murders were symbolic. He considers himself too direct a person for that. "If I had meant to kill the old man, I would have gone down and killed him."

3.

Julie Karamazov

After my second visit with Karamazov at Ionia, I went to talk with his wife Julie—she had agreed to see me. She and her children lived in a one-story frame house on Mill Street on the outskirts of Ionia, a couple of houses from the railroad track. There was a glassed-in porch along the front of the house; one window was broken and a pane was missing in the storm door. Four used automobile tires lay on the porch. The small panes in the front-door window had been painted with a stained-glass effect, except for one clear pane in the middle.

Julie Karamazov invited me into the small, neatly kept living room and introduced me to her friend Phyllis who stayed through our conversation. Julie had arranged for the children to stay with a babysitter. There were two easy chairs and a sofa in the room, and on one wall a couple of dark, skillful paintings by Luke, one of a praying girl and another of Christ, and a lively picture of the Pink Panther that he had made from the aluminum foil on candy wrappers. On another wall hung a framed photograph of Luke looking formidable in a beard, long hair, and dark glasses, and on a small table was a wedding picture taken during their prison ceremony a year and a half earlier. He was wearing the dark glasses there, too.

Julie is an attractive, direct person, easy to talk with. Dressed in slacks and a printed T-shirt, with the pink, heart-shaped watch on a chain around her neck, she looked like any neighbor, slightly plump around the middle, pretty. From her appearance, you would hardly guess the tough-ness and resilience that has carried her through a series of calamities. She brought coffee and talked about her life.

The oldest of five children, she grew up in a small house on Mt. Olivet Road in Kalamazoo Township, five houses up from the police station, not far from where the Searls lived. She went out with both of the Searl boys in high school, saw them at football games, met them at their house or at hers. She and Martha Gillman were "busy rotating back and forth between them." As she remembers it, she was always more drawn to Ralph than to Tommy. "Tommy was more outgo-ing, always chasing some skirt. Ralph was withdrawn. He sat by the window, a definite loner. Maybe he knew he had more to offer."

Julie's mother was not enthusiastic about either of the boys—or, rather, "When Tommy was around, she liked Ralph. When Ralph was around, she liked Tommy. It was whoever was there was no good." But her parents were not altogether antagonistic to the boys. Her father drove her to the bus station to say good-bye to Ralph when he left for the army and gave him train fare to come home after basic train-ing. "They wanted their daughter to go to college. They wanted more for their daughter, is what it was. I just didn't do what they had planned for me."

While they were in high school, Julie's attraction to Ralph was one sided. He was friendly enough, but he didn't really pay much attention to her. From the time he was fif-teen, he had been spending nights, whenever he could, with Betty Fitzell, a married woman ten years older than he. Julie never saw Betty Fitzell, but she heard Ralph talk about her. "My opinion is she was a bitch."

Then on the first of June, 1964, the *Gazette* carried the news that Ralph Searl had confessed to five murders. "When the news broke, my mother cried. She tried to keep us home from school. She said that it was a lie, that it wasn't true, that maybe he was saying this to get attention." Julie herself went to the Defense Attorney and offered to testify for Ralph. She went to the trial whenever she could—and she was there in the courtroom on October 7 when the jury returned the verdict, guilty of first-degree murder.

Since it seemed Ralph was gone forever, Julie took up with Tommy. The first part of the year, she lived in an apartment on Lovell Street in downtown Kalamazoo; a student-teacher picked her up each morning and took her out to Parchment High School, where she was in her senior year. Tommy began coming around to the apartment and before long moved in with her. Then they lived for a while in Tommy's apartment on Douglas Avenue. When the money ran out, Julie moved back home and finished high school in the spring.

By that time she was pregnant. When she told Tommy, he wanted to get married right away. She hesitated, then said no. Her mother approved of that decision and offered to adopt the baby if she promised not to marry Tommy.

> Then one night Tommy's mother showed up, Tommy showed up, and my mom and dad—everyone was at the house fighting about what was going to happen with *my* life. And the next day I said, "OK, I'll marry you." And Tommy went down and made arrangements for us to get married. I didn't even realize we were going to get married that day. He had the blood tests and everything run through in a big hurry. We were married by the Justice of the Peace. Spent our wedding night at his mother's house—after we'd been to Schwarz's Drive In.

There was never any doubt in Tommy's mind, she said, that she really wanted Ralph. It was a source of fights between them. The most spectacular of those fights occurred about two-and-a-half years later, when their son David was two. It was set off by letters from Ralph in prison. According to Tommy, talking about these same events with me later, two letters came in the mail from Ralph, one for Julie and one for David. Tommy opened the letter to David, thinking he would read it to him. It began "Dear David, How's my son? How's that husband of your mother's? Give your mother a kiss for me and tell her I love her." So Tommy opened the letter to Julie: "My dearest darling Julie . . ." He left the house for a time, living on the other side of town, but then came back after Julie convinced him that this passionate correspondence was Ralph's doing, not hers. But after Tommy had been back a few weeks he found in Julie's purse a letter to Ralph which began, "My dearest darling Ralph, I don't know how much longer I can put up with him."

This account is compatible with Julie's though she didn't go into detail. Tommy did find letters that Ralph had written to her. She wasn't so upset that he had found the letters, but he threatened to go to court, get a divorce, and with the evidence of the letters get custody of David. "I can remember having a heck of a fight. I was tearing the house apart looking for the hiding place where he had hid these letters." Then that furor died down. "I probably convinced him there was nothing to it, I don't know."

Then we had a fight later about money. There was a hundred and twenty bucks, I remember. I wanted to pay a bill, Tommy didn't want to pay a bill, he wanted to do some crazy thing. I went in the bedroom and called him a few dirty names. He came in after me, threw the money up in the air and started beating the hell out of me. I somehow made it to a phone and called my sister, who called my dad. My sister came over and Tommy was still beating on me. My sister grabbed a bottle and stood like this over Tommy's head and told him, "Do it again, you son of a bitch, and I'll let you have it." About this time Dad walks in and grabs

44

the bottle, you know, takes it out of Shannon's hand. Then Tommy and I are fighting about David, we are physically pulling this kid. Tommy's saying he's taking David and I'm saying, "You ain't having David." We were physically tearing the kid, pulling the kid, is what we were doing. Tommy took off, disappeared, I didn't hear a thing from him till a month later somebody called me and said there'd been a newspaper story that he was in Laramie County Jail.

She phoned and found out that Tommy had been moved to a prison in Cheyenne. At first he refused to talk with her, but then they talked, and she and Tommy's sister Leslie drove out to Wyoming to see what was happening. Tommy had taken off just as the roads were being plowed out after the great blizzard of 1967. He had headed north across the Mackinac Bridge, intending, he told them, to go to Alaska. He drove across the Upper Peninsula through Wisconsin into Minnesota. There the temperature was 61 degrees below zero, counting the wind-chill factor, and Tommy figured it would be even colder in Alaska. So, he said, he headed southwest toward Wyoming. Near the Colorado border, he picked up a teenaged boy and girl who were hitch-hiking beside their disabled car. Tommy had a pistol he had bought, thinking he would need it in Alaska, and he threatened the couple with it, tied up the boy, left him under an underpass on the road, and took the girl off to tie her up. It occurred to him that he might be getting himself in a lot of trouble, so he untied the couple, drove to the home of one of them, and turned himself in.

Why had he gone through this curious series of actions? "Tommy convinced me that he had done it because he wanted to go to jail to see if I'd wait for him. I cared so much for Ralph, maybe if *he* went to jail, I'd care for him, too." Julie was convinced it was her fault. At the preliminary hearing, she learned that rape charges had been dropped. Rape charges? Tommy hadn't told her anything about that. He was charged with kidnapping, but the sheriff assured her that since Tommy had never been in trouble before, he would get out of it. Rape charges had been dropped—evidently there was no rape. But at the trial, the judge noted the long history of trouble in Searl's family and, in order to teach him a lesson, gave him eighteen months to two years.

Julie wrote to Tommy, drove out with David to see him once, and drove out again to pick him up when he was released, after thirteen months. In the meantime, their second son, Brad, had been born. The prison psychologist in Wyoming, whom Julie had talked with several times on the phone and whose house she stayed at overnight when she went out to pick up Tommy, told her that Tommy had never known love as he was growing up. Love to him was a new shirt: when the shirt wore out, love was gone. If she could be a wife, mother, friend, and sister to Tommy, she would have the best husband in the world. "Being naive and twenty years old, I could do it, you know?"

They came back to Kalamazoo and for the next five months things seemed to be going well. "Things were falling together, we weren't fighting, we weren't having the problems. We were going out. I didn't like the way he was with David and Brad, I thought he was too stern with them. We used to argue about that, but none of the serious beating-type things were occurring. Suddenly the police knock on my door—the night I was planning on telling Tommy that Kent is on the way." Tommy was being held by the Battle Creek police on a kidnapping charge.

Tommy claimed that he had never seen the black girl whom he was accused of accosting and kidnapping. He said he had been selling vacuum sweepers at the time. He was picked up, he figured, just because he was Ralph's brother. Julie hired an attorney, who tried to convince the judge that bail should be reduced because Searl had a wife and two children, with a third on the way. (This was the first Tommy had heard of his third son.) The judge said he should have thought about all that before he committed the crime. Julie sold some of her belongings, borrowed money from Tommy's mother, and appealed to his aunt and uncle to put up some of their property as collateral. Out on bond, Tommy worked at a Tulsa gas station, "ungodly hours, eighty-some hours a week, bringing home all the money he could, paying all the bills, for a change." Julie followed the leads that Tommy had given her, visiting the homes where he had been selling vacuum cleaners at the time the abduction was supposed to have taken place. "He did tell me the truth, he had been to those houses. However, he had been to those houses in the morning not in the afternoon when the events had taken place. I questioned him about that and he said the people were wrong. He had been there in the afternoon."

Their attorney assured them that if Tommy pled guilty the judge would let him out on probation. The day of the trial, they took the children along to Battle Creek, confident that they would all be coming back together that evening. But instead of probation, the judge sentenced Searl to three to four years in prison for felonious assault. During the months that followed, Julie wrote to Tommy and visited him in Jackson Prison. It seemed to her that he became more and more critical of her. She didn't get there on time, she didn't write often enough, she didn't do what he told her to do. Suddenly she had an attack of appendicitis, went to the hospital, had her appendix out, and the next day gave birth to her third son, Kent. "I finally get up to see Tommy—the kid's nine days old—and he's cussing at me because he hadn't been notified before. He's completely incapable of thinking I'm laid up in a hospital bed. He's mad at me because I hadn't brought his son." She decided she couldn't take it any more. She started writing to Ralph and talking about divorce—with her minister, who encouraged her to leave Tommy, and with her parents, who had long been in favor of that.

I go up and see Ralph and he says, "I'm not going to tell you what to do. It's your decision. All I can do is ask you to look at the facts: you've got a horse that you know is going to win and you've got a horse over here that has lost twice. Which one are you going to bet your life on?"

The winning horse he spoke of was himself.

4.

Brothers

If Dennis Searl created an arbitrary, violent, unmanageable world for his sons while he was still with the family, he also left them a legacy of conflict that developed and came to a climax after he was gone: a ferocious competition between the two boys.

Tom was just a year older than I was, but it was emphasized, strongly. It was a strong year. It wasn't as though we were considered equals. I was always smaller than he was, a lot smaller until we got fifteen or sixteen, then I suddenly caught up with him and we pretty much stayed even. But when we were younger, he was a good head taller. The first incident I remember when he and I were together in a real sense—we were together, shooting the guns for instance, but we weren't together; I was in my world, he was in his. But the first incident, the old man was sitting up there drinking—we were sitting in the living room—and he took out a quarter and threw it in the middle of the floor. He told us to fight and whoever won got the quarter. We literally tried to kill each other, you know, over this damn quarter. Naturally Tom won, and I detested him for it, even more so because the old man grabs him and pulls him down next to him, gives him the quarter, and I'm standing there crying. Both of them, "I hate you, you bastards" because, you know, there wasn't any question about who was going to win. I definitely hated them both for it.

As with most things in Ralph's life, this competitiveness was intense, open, and long lasting, not mitigated by any restraint or pretense. It is as though each of the boys felt that his standing in the world depended on outdoing his brother. According to Becker, this is true of children generally: competition with their brothers and sisters takes on the full force of their drive for self-esteem:

> We like to speak casually about "sibling rivalry," as though it were some kind of by-product of growing up, a bit of competitiveness and selfishness of children who have been spoiled, who haven't yet grown into a generous social nature. But it is too all-absorbing and relentless to be an aberration. It expresses the heart of the creature: the desire to stand out, to be *the* one in creation. (Becker, 3)

Becker is describing what he finds a little beneath the surface in most children, disguised by the affection they know they are *supposed* to feel (and in fact *do* feel) toward their brothers and sisters and by the self-control their parents urge on them almost from the year of their birth. But instead of urging self-control on his sons, Dennis Searl pushed them into open battle with each other. As they grew older the battle continued as fierce and blatant as when they were fighting for their father's quarter on the floor, but more deadly. Once when the children, then in high school, were home alone, they fought about doing the dishes. Tommy threw a salad bowl at Leslie, and Ralph threw a steak knife at Tommy. The knife hit him on the forehead, handle first, scaring them both—but not enough to prevent their fighting even more ferociously a few years later.

Tommy, now in Marquette prison, says, "Ralph was the only companion I had most of my life. He's the only true foe I've ever had in my life. He's the only competition I've ever had in my life." This competition reached a fierce pitch in a shooting incident when the boys had become men, eighteen and nineteen years old. Each of them tells about it with a strange intensity as though it had just happened.

Ralph's account is the shorter of the two. In it, the object of the fight was Julie:

> I was eighteen at the time. It was after I got out of the army, just before I started shooting people, a couple of months before that, maybe six months. What happened is, Tom was in the navy, so I had taken one of his girls away from him—he was engaged to this girl and I moved in on her, took his ring off and put it in the drawer, and it was her and I. He came out on leave, and I didn't particularly care about the girl. It was one of the rare times we came together as allies: both of us dropped the broad at the same time, which crushed her.
>
> Then when he went back to the navy, he was going with Julie, but she still had this thing for me. While he was gone, I started going with her, and one day I came in from work or somewhere, drove up to the house, and walked up towards the back door. I didn't know there was anything going on, but just as I got to the door he comes out and kicks me in the nuts. Naturally it laid me out.
>
> As soon as I could walk again, I got up, went in the bedroom and got this pistol that I had, the one that I started killing people with. It was him and a buddy of his, they were in the house at the

time. So I came out of the bedroom and pointed the pistol at him. I was still hurting, you know; we could hardly talk to each other, so I said, "You son of a bitch. I'm going to kill you, boy."

Well, he thought I was playing. And I didn't really want to kill him, you know? What I wanted to do was scare him, make him know how close he had come. So what I did, I had it on his face and I moved it over and shot past his ear. It went through the wall and out the screen door. At that point he didn't realize—he thought it was a blank. We ended up going through a wrestling match for the gun. I suppose it was lucky we didn't one of us get killed in that. But his buddy told him to forget it, and they took off. And then—well, that was the end of it, but it was dramatic for Julie because she was the object of the fury. See, we've had a history of—I've done more to him than he's done to me, but it's always been a very violent history. I used to hit him with boards, throw knives at him, shoot him with bows and arrows, and shit like that.

In Tommy's account, the episode takes on a different character. The fight was occasioned by another girl, not Julie, and Ralph is the jealous lover displaced by Tommy. The story has a different hero here, but the competitive fury between the brothers is as clear as ever:

My next boot camp leave, we had another big row. We had this thing. Julie was with *me* when I was home on leave and would write to me, write love letters and stuff. But when I came home, I found her with *him*. Plus this other girl, Martha Gillman, I found her there with him. So he's thinking he really pulled a coup on me, he's taken my girls away while I was gone. So I took Julie out, out in the garage, and told her, "Look, either you're with me or you're with him. One or the other.

Either way." So she said, "Well, I'm with you."
She said, "I won't have anything to do with him."
So I said, "OK, fine." That was the start of my
problems with Julie and him. That was just the
start of it.

So, anyway, I did the same thing to Martha
Gillman. Well, Martha stayed there. Julie went
home. My mother was gone. It was just Ralph
there and I and my buddy Jack and Martha Gillman. We went over across the street to my buddy's
house. Ralph was mad; he was home by himself.
He wouldn't have anything to do with Martha because she told him she was with me, she didn't
want to be with him. So Ralph come out of the
house yelling, "I'm going to kill you, you son of a
bitch, I'm going to kill you." He come across the
yard. Well, I met him in our front lawn and I said,
"Look, man, she don't want to be with you, she's
with me. I don't know what you want to do about
it, but that's the way it is."

He started swinging. I was going to fight him
clean. Rules of Hoyle and all this, just fight. Neither
one of us laid a glove on the other. We respected
each other too much. Stand back. Then he decided
he would go ahead and throw a little dirty stuff at
me, and he tried to kick me in the nuts. It took me by
surprise and I reared back. I was faster than he was;
Ralph was always heavier than I was. I reared back
so he hit me in the hip. I said, "Whoa, you want to
do that!" So I started sparring a little bit and ya! I hit
him right in the nuts. And that was it. He went into
a crouch and started crying, went into the house. I
could hear him in the bedroom crying. It was sum-
mertime with the windows open and all that. I
could hear him crying in there, sobbing and stuff.

My buddy said, "Well, you got him." And I
said, "Yea, but wait a minute, he'll be back." I

waited a second and then I heard, "You son of a bitch. I'm going to kill you." And he starts coming through the house. I met him right in the front lawn and we went at it again and I kicked him again. Down he went. Back in the house, crying. I think he came back out and did it again, I'm not sure. It was at least twice. Might have been three times, the same thing. I think it was three times. The third time I knew it was going to be a different story. By then Martha Gillman was crying over in the lot; she knows we're fighting over her.

My buddy said, "Well, is he going to come back out again?" And I said, "Yeah, but I don't know. I'm kind of worried because he's got that pistol in there." Then I heard what I was listening for. I heard that dresser drawer open, where he kept that pistol. I said "He's after that pistol." Jack looked at me and said, "Are you serious?" "Yea, he's after that pistol, wait and see." Jack and I started to go in the door to the kitchen. Right when we went through the door to the kitchen, Ralph came through the living room, and we met right in the doorway, the doorway of the dining room-kitchen. Ralph's got that pistol in his hand. He's shaking all over the place, so mad he can't even hold it steady. He said, "I'm going to kill you, you son of a bitch. I'm going to kill you." And he kept waving that pistol around, waving it around. And I thought, he's got blanks in that, he's trying to scare me. So I told him that. I said, "You wouldn't shoot your brother. You haven't got the balls to shoot your brother." And I started walking towards him.

Now, I'm on the left, my buddy's on the right. We just went through the doorway and spread out a little bit. Ralph's looking dead at me. He don't care about Jack, I'm the one he's shooting. He put the pistol, pointed it in my face and, bam, shot the pistol. I felt the powder hit my face. I thought blanks, he's trying to scare me. And I kept going at him. Through the living room, around the corner, down the hallway, past the bedroom doors, into the bathroom, and he's up against the wall in the bath tub, with the pistol in his hand. He's still shaking, he's scared. What I don't know at the time, he had already shot one or two guys, and he thinks that now he has shot his Nemesis, the guy he has fought with all his life. He's shot him and he's still walking at him. That scared him. That scared him, he was pure white.

Jack said, "I'll tell you what. Why don't you go on outside and I'll get the gun and the bullets away from him." See, I wasn't going to leave till I'd got the gun and the bullets. I said, "All right, that sounds cool." I could see that Ralph was completely wiped out. I had won the battle and that was it. So I walked back out of the room. Jack took the bullets from Ralph, from the gun. Let Ralph keep the gun, but he took the bullets, the shells. I walk back through the living room into the dining room and kitchen, and when I walked through the doorway from the dining room into the kitchen, I just froze. I took a step backwards. I looked back up and there was a bullet hole clean through that wall. It went through the wall and right out the screen door. My knees turned to jelly, because I knew then that he'd really shot a shell.

I've thought maybe that was one reason he shot those other people in the back of the head like that—so they wouldn't keep tracking him, keep coming at him. He shot the rest of them in the back of the head, see. I mean, that was the first and last time he ever shot anybody's face.

It is probably impossible to discover, at this distance, where the truth may lie in these two accounts. And in any case the truth or falsehood of the details is not the point.

What is unmistakable is the intensity of the rivalry between the two brothers. Even now, fifteen years after the event, these two men in their thirties are reliving the antagonism that was the central fact of their childhood, each stealing the girl from his brother, each emerging as hero. It is as though each feels he has been robbed by his brother of the thing most precious to him, and he must steal it back, in fact or in imagination, if it takes the rest of his life.

Ralph is skeptical of the psychiatrist's hypothesis that in these murders he was symbolically killing his father, and I have little desire to argue that he was symbolically killing his brother. Still, Tommy's inclination to connect the near-murder of a brother with the real murders that occurred a few months later has some plausibility. Probably in some sense Ralph's Nemesis, his unkilled brother, did keep tracking him during the months of the murders.

Possibly, in an even more direct way, Ralph was present at Tommy's murders, eight years later. As it happened, Tommy was released from Jackson Prison on February 17, 1972, just when Ralph was being returned first to Jackson and then to the Kalamazoo County Jail to await retrial. Kalamazoo had not paid much attention to Tommy's crimes; his assaults had been committed in other cities and he was tried elsewhere. But when Ralph came back to town, the Kalamazoo *Gazette* carried articles recalling his murders and his trial and recapitulating the progress of his appeal. The city was aware that one of its most notorious criminals was back. Here is Julie's account of the months after Tommy's release from Jackson:

> So then, Tommy comes back from Jackson in February. First night he was home, he came over to pick the boys up—I allowed him to see the boys— and we didn't hardly speak to each other. Then one day he called me and asked me if I want to see Ralph. I said, yes, I was making arrangements to go to Jackson to see him. He said, "You don't have

to go to Jackson. Ralph's coming down here to Kalamazoo." I hung up the phone and I can still remember standing there at that phone. A girl friend of mine was there at the time, and I said, "There's going to be trouble." She said, "What?" I said, "They cannot bring Ralph back for trial and just release Tommy from Jackson and not expect trouble. There's going to be trouble." Lo and behold, there was trouble.

Twice Tommy took me up to see Ralph. It was during this second ride home from the jail seeing Ralph that I got this gut instinct, I had this feeling that Tommy had committed murder. I had no tangible proof, I had nothing to go to the authorities with, but I knew it. There was no doubt in my mind, I knew it. I went home and talked to some friends about it and they told me I was crazy. I had looked for trouble since the day I had hung up that phone, and I was seeing something that wasn't there. So from March until July, he was seeing the kids. He would be there like clockwork every other weekend. In July one weekend he didn't pick the kids up. I thought, well, that's strange. He didn't call or anything. A couple of days later I read some stuff in the newspaper, I went back to my calendar, and I knew it again. I had no proof, but I knew it. I knew where he'd been that weekend he hadn't picked up the boys. I called the prosecutor and told him to check the whereabouts of Tommy, but didn't leave my name, didn't do anything else about it. Then at that point I stopped listening to the news, stopped getting the newspaper or anything.

Eventually, the jury convicted Tommy of the rape and murder, committed on March 18, of Cynthia Kohls, who was returning with her two-year-old son to her car after shopping at a discount store in town. In July, two young women from Chicago, driving through Kalamazoo on their way to Ann Arbor, stopped at the gas station where Searl and a friend were working. Their bodies were found near Kilowatt Lake, raped and murdered. A fourth girl was found murdered near the same lake before Searl's friend confessed and Searl was arrested.

I asked Julie why she foresaw trouble as soon as she heard that the brothers would both be in Kalamazoo in February.

> Tommy could not stand the thought—even during Ralph's trial when all the publicity was going on— Tommy hated this, he hated the thought that his brother was getting this publicity. And I knew that he was disturbed and confused enough that with Ralph's appeal coming up again, he would not be able to handle this publicity thing, that he would have to do something to put himself in the limelight. They were always, both of them, they were both very, very, competitive.

5.

Dark Glasses

As I made trips to Ionia to interview Karamazov, his wife, and others associated with him, I was troubled sometimes to think that I was contributing to the pleasure and importance he felt because of his murders. It was a heady feeling, he said, for a nineteen-year-old boy to enter prison as a notorious murderer. Similarly, the ego must enjoy a small lift to have a grown man drive two hours to record his words. There was no avoiding the truth that I was there because he was a murderer. If he had just been a high school dropout and a poor soldier, I would not even have driven across Kalamazoo to talk with him.

I wondered how much his day-by-day life in prison depended on his reputation as a murderer. Could he still live on that fame?

> No, but you know it's valuable even today. People won't approach me like they approach other people. For instance, in here, there's a really drastic racial problem. Racial tension is right at its peak all the time. Yet I can freely float from one element to another; most of the spades are just literally terrified of me. Last night on the rock there was a little

59

fish that moved in a couple of cells down. I happened to be the only honky within, oh, twenty-five cells either way. So he gets to talking about honkies and pretty soon he gets to talking about me. I start getting ready to check him and the guy on the other side of him checks him. "Hey, you better leave that guy alone, the sucker will come out and kill you in the morning." Boom, the guy shuts right up. And that's the end of that; he will never say another word to me or about me or anything else.

But usually, they're just talking about honkies as though they're a piece of shit, you know. They've got that group thing, they ride in packs. I've been in Recreation two years, and honkies just don't stay in Recreation. That's the dog hang-out, the boxers and strong arm guys, that's their assignment really. I've been there a year and there has been no problem. I've had a couple of almost fights, but somebody buzzed them up in time to stop it. That's something—you can't really give it up, you know?

He clearly takes pride in his reputation, which extends beyond the prison into the town of Ionia. His wife Julie reports to him the rumors she hears and overhears downtown.

Ask Julie about that. They've got me having killed up to fifty people. They've got me as a Mafia hit man. Every story you get downtown is different. These cops will go down to the bar and get half looped and start talking about me, and the next thing you know everybody in town is believing that I'm some kind of a raving maniac. It gets her down, too, when she finds out about it. Someone will say to her, "Aren't you married to the guy who killed thirty-five people?" She gets a little upset about it.

She gets upset, perhaps, but his voice suggests little chagrin on his part.

In fact, he takes some pains to preserve this aura of strangeness and danger. That is where the dark glasses come in.

> The Inspector asked me six or eight months ago, he said, "Hey, why don't you take off your glasses as a first step to letting us know you're a different person?" I said, "No way." Because if I take off these glasses, the mystery is gone. I invite people to try me. Right now, I'm the fastest gun in town, and as long as I've got these on, they don't know if my hand has slowed down or not. If I take them off, then the first time I get mad at somebody, it shows. My eyes get icy cold when I get mad—I don't get mad, really, I get cold. Now if someone sees that, sees me get mad like that, and I don't take the next ultimate step, where am I at then? The next time somebody walks by, "He won't do nothing anyway. Do what you want to do." And there I am. With these things on, I haven't had to kill anybody yet, I haven't had to do anything.

6.

Moving toward Murder

Even in a childhood made fierce by competition with his brother and by fear of his father, there were times and places that Ralph Searl remembers with satisfaction.

I loved school, other than the fact of little kids making fun. But I loved school, and I was good at it—in the early years, I was good in school. In third grade, we had this teacher, Mrs. Marquardt, Mrs. Nellie Marquardt—a big, heavy woman, a farm woman. In her class, every day, we had a crafts period. She'd bring in wood and saws and nails and hammers, and she'd let us pick out something we wanted to make—a birdhouse or a tray. I loved that, that was the most tremendous thing in school. I made a birdhouse the first time and everybody said it was so *good*, you know. It *was*, it was decent—as I remember it. I loved that class and went through it with flying colors.

I talked with Mrs. Marquardt, now retired, and she confirmed Ralph's impression: they did make birdhouses and Ralph did pretty well that year, though she can't pick his birdhouse out from the others in her memory. Ironically, he was reminded just then of his powerlessness.

63

We got to the end of the year, and I don't
know what possessed Mom to tell me, but Tom
flunked the fourth grade and they said, "Well,
what we'll do is we'll keep you back so you don't
catch up with him. That would make him feel
bad." And from that day on until the day I left
school, I never once ever did anything in school
again. Absolutely nothing. I'm a little third grader,
and to this day I so distinctly remember thinking,
"Fuck it. If that's the way it is, what I've done is
totally irrelevant to the whole thing. You're just
going to slap me down." I remember saying to hell
with it, there's just not . . . there's no fairness in
the world, I suppose, was the feeling.

There is also one place that, even now, Ralph thinks of
with unqualified contentment, a farm owned by Ben Barrett,
his mother's supervisor at Kalamazoo Valley Paper. The Bar-
retts, probably guessing the boy's need to be part of another
family, invited him to spend summers and weekends there,
and he did that for three or four years, beginning shortly
after his father left, when he was eleven.

I think that was the first time I started enjoying things. What it was, it was usually the solitude
that I enjoyed. I lived in the basement and I had a
fireplace and the whole shot down there. Really it
was an unfinished basement, but they had a fireplace there, and bunk beds. I'd build a fire, then I'd
just sit, you know, and watch the flames. After
work, I'd go out and—usually just go out and
tramp around there. When I finally got my shotgun, I'd wander around in the woods. That's
where I came to like solitude, I guess. Everything
that was good out there was associated with solitude. Even the work—I enjoyed it but the older
guys that I worked with, you know, they were the
kind of people that just had to have nicknames,

usually derogatory. I was *chipmunk* to this one particular guy. Every time I'd work around him, I'd be
chipmunk and *little bastard* and all that. So I didn't
particularly enjoy working around him, whereas if
I was allowed to work on my own, then it was fine.
I was trusted out there; that was the big plus factor.

Even there I was put in competition with
Tom. The drive was so great to show him up, I
suppose, that I didn't want him out there; I wanted
him out of the setting. So I was Johnny-on-the-
spot, I was the first one up in the morning. He'd
never get up. We'd be out working two or three
hours before he'd ever get up. Eventually, I out-
shone him so tough that they just said to hell with
it, and started leaving him home and taking me out
there alone. I was supremely happy then. In fact, I
hated it when Mom or any of the other kids would
come—they'd come out on weekends once in a
while. It would detract from my own enjoyment of
it; I loathed them even coming. I suppose I wanted
to push them away. But the farm was thoroughly
enjoyable. Even the bad experiences, you know,
like getting run over by the tractor and all that—
even that made it strangely better. During the
school year, I'd have to come in, Monday morning.
I always hated coming back to town.

If this were a Dickens novel, this idyll on the farm near
Scotts, Michigan, coinciding, by luck, with the years of
Ralph's coming of age, would have made all the difference.
Mr. Barrett even had a daughter, Sarah, a year or two older
than Ralph; the two of them were inseparable, brother and
sister. Sarah had a horse, and Ralph remembers one day the
horse brushed her off on a tree, so that she fell on the grass,
her nose bloodied. As he ran to help her up, he became
terrified, thinking of his mother bleeding on the white bed-
spread. He cried, and afterwards tried to explain to her what

had happened earlier and how her blood recalled the terror of the bedroom where he "saw red." One could easily expand upon this scene: Sarah, amazed at first by the violence of the boy's reaction, would listen as he reached back into the past and explained his feelings to her and to himself. She would begin to understand the aloofness that had puzzled her. Bound by blood, they would eventually fall in love.

Thinking back to his farm visits, Ralph says, "They had such a close family relationship that I would set back and see all that I had missed. At some point in there I said, 'Oh, these things are what I need: these relationships, these values, these demands.'" It sounds like the turning point in a romantic story. But Dickens didn't write this plot. During these same years when Ralph was spending summers and weekends on the farm, he served as a safety patrol at school and extorted milk money from the kids who passed his corner. Of himself and his friends at school, he says, "We were young hoodlums, is what we were."

In eighth grade, shortly after the farm years, he got in a fight with the science teacher.

> He was one of these sons of bitches—what he'd do, if he caught you talking in class, he'd tell you to put your head down in your arms. And then he'd sneak up behind you, and if he saw you peeking, you know, if you had your eyes above arm level, he'd come and bust you on the back of the head. He was bloodying girls' noses and everything else, pushing their faces into the desk. So he tried that crap on me. "Put your head on the desk."
>
> I said, "No, no way."
>
> "You're going to put your head on the desk."
>
> "Kiss my ass."
>
> "What did you say?"
>
> "Kiss my ass." So he grabbed me by the collar, you know, from behind, and I was standing there, damn near as big as he was. He yanked me

up out of the chair and then grabbed me by the front of the shirt. And he caught himself trying to drag me out of the class. I said, "I'm not going nowhere." I told him to get his fucking hands off me, or something. So he slaps me across the face.

"Say it again, I'll slap you again."

"Fuck you."

Bang he slaps me again, so it ended up he slapped me ten or twelve times, back and forth, till he had my nose bleeding on both sides, my lips were all cut, blood all over his shirt and everything. And I still, you know, there's no way in the world I'm going to apologize or quit saying what I'm saying.

Searl must have been fourteen when he and the science teacher went to it. The tough resentful belligerence of that episode, his refusal to quit saying what he was saying, was characteristic of Searl, or of one part of him, in the years that followed—and is still characteristic now.

At the same time he does seem to be capable of affection, or at least headlong devotion to a woman. When he was still only fourteen, he began seeing Betty Fitzell, a woman ten years older than he was, a slim, well-built Hungarian woman, formerly an Arthur Murray dance instructor. By the time he was fifteen, he would sneak over to her house after her husband went to work at 11:00 P.M. and spend the night with her. She had three children, adorable, as Searl remembers them, and adoring toward him. When he was sixteen, Searl quit school and Betty Fitzell got divorced, so he moved in with her, baby-sitting and doing some of the housework while she was at work. But he had not been domesticated: he and another boy stole a car and were caught.

The judge gave Searl the option of going into the juvenile home or into the army. He chose the army, enlisting the day he turned seventeen. "I went in all enthusiastic: I was going to be a lifer, that's what I was going to be." He asked to be assigned to an airborne company—and was for a month or so. This was during the time of the Bay of Pigs fiasco. At first the army increased its airborne troops dramatically, but then, when the emergency had passed, they sent hundreds of recruits in for repeat physical examinations. Searl was reassigned because of trick knees.

Then what they did was they kept me in a shipping and receiving company for like three months. They wouldn't give me any orders. It was a punitive type thing. So I fell in with this—no, what really set it off, it was Christmas time and I didn't have money enough to get a ticket and they wouldn't loan me any money to go home. Well, we started drinking heavy on the base, Fort Benning, Georgia. We were drinking every night, down at the service club, 3.2 beer. We'd drink pitcher after pitcher of that shit, there was four or five of us. And they had these little bags of Wise potato chips. I just loved these damn things. So I'd eat them all night, and I'd buy two bags to take back to the barracks with me. Then I'd go down and take a shower, come back and get in bed, eat those two bags of chips, and fall out.

But one particular night, I went through this routine. I go down to take a shower—but when I come back, they're gone. There's about ten or twelve guys around, we're up on the second floor. So I'm drunker than hell. Where are my chips at? Well, this little clown, he was a short little dude, he's over on the other side of the room, talking about he ate them. You little son of a bitch—I started chasing him around the barracks. The more I chased him around, they kicked footlockers in front of me and everything else, so big joke.

Finally him and this other guy fly down the stairs, and I'm chasing right after them. I come running down to the barracks door and they disappear, I can't find them. So I'm hotter than hell now. I'm really pissed. Looking for them, I end up down in officers' country, by their dining hall. So I put my fist through the window—you know, the door was locked—cut myself all to hell on my knuckle and everything, and I break into the place. There was a big cake there—it must have been Christmas or New Year's—there was this big, huge cake setting on the table. So I hit the icing on it one time. Then I pulled open this drawer in the table and it's all full of knives. I took two great big old butcher knives, must have been eighteen, twenty inches long, each, great big heavy ones.

I come by there and I'm dripping blood all over hell. What I did, right here, it sliced all that scar right there. See, the window caught that knuckle there and, pshoo, peeled it all right back, but I didn't feel anything now, I was so drunk. So I started looking for these guys, this one in particular. Finally I found them. They were between the barracks, walking down between this line of barracks. I sneak up behind them. I had the knives like this, you know? across my chest. When I got right up to them, I was going to come around and hit both of them, on the side of their neck. I pulled the knives apart, and they clanged, you know they came together, and boy, those guys took off like a shot.

So I'm chasing them all over this whole damn area. Finally, they come back down through the barracks, and here's this whole group of guys, thirty or forty guys there, with the sergeant in front of them, and they all got mop handles and brooms and all this in their hands. So, probably bravado again, I walked right up to all of them: "Now what you want to do?"

"Just give us the knives and everything will be all right."

I said, "I'll give you the knives!" Whish. I took a swing at them. I don't know if I wanted to hit them or not, but they all ducked and off into the woodwork they went. So I'm running all over this whole company area here, down to the airport and everything else. Pretty soon they call the MP's in. They got MP's all over the area, in these old Chevies, lights on and all, looking for me.

For some reason I go over to the orderly room, kick the door in, and they're sitting there playing poker. So I go in and drop these two knives on this glass desk top, and they all cream their jeans right there. All right, I turn in the knives and they take me up to the hospital. They told the doctor—you know, he wanted to put some pain killer or something on it while he sewed it up—"He don't need nothing, he's a tough guy. Just sew him up." So the god damn doctor is going through with the needle, no kind of anesthesia or anything. They bring me back and they put me in the barracks again, under secure wraps. They bring me up on charges of assault with intent to do grave bodily harm including murder, give me a general court martial.

The army assigned Searl a lawyer and kept his court martial pending for two or three months. Meanwhile, he was not locked up. Free to go his own way, he got in with a group of enlisted men who were stealing clothes and anything else they could find from the cars of men who were taking officer's training.

So, what really got me cracked was a guy who came in the shipping and receiving company. He was laying out there sleeping. He had a hell of a radio—AM, FM, short wave, the whole bit—setting between his feet. He was laying on the bed with his feet up on the foot locker, the radio between them, sleeping, waiting for his bus. So this monkey comes to me and he says—he knew I was dealing in hot shit—"You want the radio?"

"Yeah."

"Give me two dollars, OK?"

"You got it coming."

So he sneaks over there and steals this guy's radio, brings it back to me, I give him two bucks, and put it in the foot locker. I had four or five foot lockers, clothing bags, and the racks behind the bunks, these are all full of army clothes, civilian clothes, you know, everything imaginable.

Now just before this, there was a sergeant who was transferred out. While he was packing his shit in the trunk—I hated this bastard because he was always on my tail—while he was packing his shit, going from the barracks to the car, he left the trunk open. So I'm out there just standing around and I see this pistol in the back of his trunk, a .22 Ruger Bearcat with a holster and all that. He goes back in the barracks, whishoo, I snatch it and pack it in the chimney [an abandoned chimney stack standing near the barracks]. He never even noticed. He packed up his shit and left. This is how I get the pistol that I eventually started popping people with.

Finally, the army police shook down the barracks and found the cache of stolen goods behind Searl's bunk. Besides that, they caught the "monkey" who stole the radio.

The monkey's confessed everything. Yeah, he stole it, but I told him to steal it and offered him money to steal it, etc., so the MP calls me in the sergeant's office, confronts me with this evidence, you know. I don't know what he's talking about. He says, "Well"—he looks at his watch. It was, I don't know, quarter to four or something. He says, "I'm putting you under CQ arrest," which I was under already. This means you're confined to the barracks, is all it is. "I'll be back in the morning to take you to the stockade, grand larceny."

"OK."

So he leaves at five of four or so, he splits. Gives orders to the sergeant, you know, to put me under CQ arrest. The sergeant left at about ten after four. At four thirty, I left.

It must be clear by now that Searl shows many of the characteristics of the psychopathic personality. For example, he acts impulsively with no sense of his own long-range comfort or safety, flying into an almost murderous rage over two bags of Wise potato chips or filling foot lockers with stolen goods, leaving them where they will surely be discovered in time—without even caring much about the items that he steals. Or, again, he seems completely free of nervousness or anxiety, never deeply bothered by regret or shame, even when he has just been caught stealing or when he is telling me that he extorted milk money from children on their way to school. In the episodes we have looked at, and especially in the ones that follow, we see another characteristic quality, an almost incredible ability to charm people and inspire trust in them. As though they were enchanted, people treat him tenderly, hardly able to believe ill of him: the military police do not find it necessary to lock him up, and the Texas Rangers seem persuaded by a touching story, fabricated on the spot, about the dangers of travel. And after all this—well, Searl will tell it:

I went AWOL, went to Mexico. I took the pistol with me. It ended up the border patrol got me in Nuevo Laredo, down in Mexico, just across the border from Laredo, Texas. They thought I was a post office robber. They gave me a shakedown on the highway there and when they opened up my

AWOL bag, this loaded .22 pistol falls out. Setting right on top. So they take me into the station and they found—I had them all convinced that I was just a kid hitch-hiking. They had already made up their minds I probably wasn't the damn post office robber, but one of these clowns was looking at all the pictures of broads in my wallet. I had my ID card stuck way up in behind, and he happened to find that. So right in the middle of my story—I'm telling, you know, this big, long, sad story about how a kid can't be too careful on the highway, and perverts and all that—and he finds the ID card. "You're AWOL from the army."

"Yeah, I know."

They put me in the stockade, the air force stockade in Texas, and then they gave me a general order to return to Fort Benning, Georgia. Really, it's just an order, but if you disobey a general order, it's supposed to be very severe. They gave me train tickets and food coupons and all that to cover me back to Georgia, put me on a train, and away I went. So I came back and they threw me in the stockade, gave me a general court martial—six months in the stockade, two-thirds loss of pay, etc. I ended up doing ninety-two days. It was unreal, you know what they did? I do ninety-two, ninety-three days in the stockade. They're going to discharge me, so they let me out of the stockade, give me my clothes, what was left of them, what hadn't been stolen, then they give me my back pay, and they give me the *pistol*. They put me on the bus back to Michigan. This is how I come to have this damn pistol. They just gave it back to me, you know? I suppose they had to; they never knew it was stolen. That was what started it all. Finally, I got a pistol, now what am I going to do with it.

7.

Friends in Ionia

Karamazov's assurance that I need only ask for Deputy Warden Leonard Jespersen or Director of Treatment Glen Langdon and all doors would open implies a good deal of confidence in his standing with the top officials in the Michigan Reformatory at Ionia. Clearly he believed that if the Deputy Warden knew I was coming to see Karamazov, he would personally see to it that I was admitted promptly. I had no occasion to test Karamazov's closeness to the staff in just this way, but my conversations with Jespersen, Langdon, and James Russell, Director of Recreation in the prison, lead me to believe that his prediction about the doors opening was accurate, at least in October 1976 when that letter was written. A few months later, Karamazov felt that he had been betrayed by the staff in a marijuana episode and, indignant, he took his case to the state prison officials in Lansing, causing considerable commotion at Ionia and angering people there. We will look at that incident toward the end of the book, but for the moment, yes, Karamazov was unusually close to the top staff at Ionia.

For two years, until December 1976 when he became an assistant in Hobby Craft, Karamazov was a clerk in Recreation. The person in charge there was James Russell, a handsome black man from Mississippi, married, with children almost ready for college. He was a high school teacher and coach before coming to Ionia ten years earlier. At first he coached football and basketball in the prison, but then he was promoted to Director of Recreation and had to give up coaching. He missed it.

Russell's office was a cubicle with windows on all sides, inside a large recreation room in the prison. Outside the cubicle were four or five well-used billiard tables. When I was there, a crew of prisoners was shampooing the indoor-outdoor carpet. When Russell led me to his desk in the center of the cubicle, he asked the men who were standing around there to leave so that we could talk privately. Most of them did, but one man stayed, going about his business on the other side of the cubicle—checking in equipment, perhaps—and others came in and out from time to time. It was clear that Russell had a relaxed relationship with the men, expecting cooperation from them but not standing on protocol. We talked about Luke, while other prisoners, I suspect, listened in on bits of the conversation.

Before he came to Recreation, Karamazov had been editor of the newspaper published by the prison school. He insisted, Russell said, on carrying his camera all over the prison and writing articles critical of the way things were done. Finally, the principal of the school said, "Either he goes or I go." Karamazov went, and most supervisors were not inclined to hire him because of the aggressiveness of his reporting and editorial writing, and because of the dark glasses he wore even then. They made people uneasy. But Russell hired him and he became "one of the most efficient clerks I've had, one of the most honest." Russell felt himself "covered with paperwork" in his job as Director of Recreation and he was grateful to Karamazov for relieving him of much of the onerous memo writing. Karamazov wrote well and could take over some administrative chores such as deciding which of the prisoners would get passes to come to Recreation. He would make out the list and hand it to Russell for his approval. I spoke with Russell two months after

76

Karamazov had moved to Hobby Craft and he obviously missed him. "When Kar was here, I could tell him what to say and he'd lay the memo on my desk. Beautiful. Or he'd see something that needed to be done and write the memo and show it to me. 'I thought this is what you'd want to say. If it's not right I'll do it again.' Now I have to write it out, then argue with them about the spelling—and they spend half a day redoing it."

But their friendship, Russell felt, was more than just the attachment between an efficient clerk and a grateful supervisor. They had long discussions about religion, Russell the churchgoer and Karamazov the atheist each trying to convince the other. When Karamazov planned to marry Julie, Russell debated with him about it. He wanted to know why, what good was it to be married and in prison? But he admired Karamazov's determination to make something new, even though he knew he might be locked up the rest of his life. He never caught him with anything illegal on the job, though he was aware that Karamazov was sending out considerable sums of money to Julie and her family—on the order of $700 over a five-month period. It is not possible to make that sort of money on a prison job so he must have been lending money or dealing in marijuana. (The usury rates in prison are extraordinary: as much as two for one, to be repaid in *two weeks*, if you can collect it.) Russell knew Karamazov must be having other people, probably staff, hold some of his money for him (in the form of prison tokens) because it is illegal to have more than $60 in your possession at one time. When I spoke with Russell, Karamazov had already been busted and put in detention for possession of marijuana, and Russell was remarkably candid—downright incautious, I thought—in telling me that he was being locked up unjustly. In any case, it was clear that he felt admiration and personal attachment to Karamazov that went well beyond the ordinary relationship between staff and prisoner.

I had a similar feeling in talking with Glen Langdon, Director of Treatment, that same morning in February 1977—a feeling that he was taking a considerable risk in talking with me as openly as he did, and that this risk was taken almost as a sign of his loyalty to Karamazov. Though he was hesitant to talk about the marijuana episode until he saw that I already knew, in general, what had happened, he then talked quite freely about it. He told me that Karamazov *had* been betrayed by prison officials in the marijuana bust, that he had been working with one of the inspectors to get evidence that could be used to convict large-scale drug dealers within the prison. Langdon told me that he himself had served as an intermediary between the Inspector and Karamazov.

Langdon, a big white man, seemed to me intelligent and direct, a psychologist whom anyone would feel comfortable talking to. I got the impression that honesty came naturally to him. He told me that according to the record Karamazov was "a real pisser" when he first came to Ionia. He had spent two years in detention, that is in solitary confinement, at Marquette. Now he had more control of himself. He had become sophisticated about the running of the prison—an inmate politician, one of ten or twelve residents who were looked on as leaders and therefore could help keep order. The other inmates, Langdon said, liked Karamazov or feared him, he didn't know which.

James Russell had told me that Karamazov would have nothing to gain by cooperating with the Inspector or the Deputy Warden—he was just doing it for the good of the cause. But, as Langdon made clear, his motives were more subtle than that. Because he was older than most of the prisoners at Ionia and had been there longer, because he was analytical and articulate as few of the other prisoners were, because he was respected by other inmates and moved freely among the leaders of the black and Puerto Rican groups, and because from time to time he provided the staff reliable information about who had guns or narcotics or where there might be a riot, he could get to see the Deputy Warden, the Inspector, or the Director of Treatment whenever he asked to see them. And this carried other satisfactions with it. The guards, for example, were often suspicious of him and a little deferential because he seemed to know the regulations and the upper echelons of the staff better than they did. They *asked* him to get a haircut instead of ordering him. He could sometimes make phone calls out or arrange extra visits, favors that would be denied to other prisoners. Ordinarily, no one checked too carefully to see what he might have in his cell. No one asked questions about the money he sent out to his wife. He got passes to move from one section of the prison to another, even in the evening when prisoners are generally locked up.

Glen Langdon was aware that Karamazov could calculate other people's needs and reactions to within a hair's breadth in order to get something he wanted. Less trusting than Russell, he knew that Karamazov's services as an informer were not offered only for the good of the cause. But apparently his skepticism did not extend to his own relationship with Luke. He considered him a friend and believed they had developed a good deal of trust. "As far as I know, he has never lied to me. I've done what I can to make his time a little easier. Sometimes it's just a matter of having a place to ventilate." Sometimes he did Karamazov more substantial favors than that, too, and received some gifts from him, not calculating any quid pro quo. When he was being the psychologist, he could describe Karamazov's shrewd detachment, but when he spoke as a friend, the tone changed. He sounded more like a teacher praising his most apt and perceptive student. He felt pride in the reasonableness and control Karamazov showed in Ionia in contrast to his cold defiance at Marquette, even though he knew that control could not be trusted completely. If I interpreted his tone of voice correctly, he felt that a bond existed between them, well beyond the bond of counselor and inmate: however impersonal Luke might be in his dealings with others, his friendship with Langdon was knit of stronger threads than convenience and calculation. Nevertheless, a month later Glen Langdon, because of his friendship with Luke, was out of a job. Luke explained that series of events to me, showing no glimmer of regret or loss.

8.

Murder

When he was back from the army, in the fall of 1963, Searl turned his ferocious energy toward Betty Fitzell, the woman he had been living with before he left. He apparently could shift from one sort of heroics to another, as long as his role was dramatic and intense. Now, in place of the aggressive bravado of his year and a half in the army, he substituted a devotion to Mrs. Fitzell that she must have found oppressive in its single-mindedness.

While he had been in the army, Betty Fitzell had got in the habit of dating, going out to nightclubs with various men. But Searl, only nineteen, could not get into nightclubs because the drinking age in Michigan then was twenty-one years. Though he was insanely jealous and "all pressure to get married," he let her go out with other men while he stayed home taking care of her children and doing housework. When he turned twenty-one, she told him, *he* could take her out dancing. "It seemed a God-awful long way away."

All that fall, he worked at odd jobs and refused to spend anything. Early in December he began buying lavish gifts for Mrs. Fitzell and her children—a vacuum cleaner, toys, and clothes. He was going to make that Christmas the best one they had ever had. But a couple of weeks before Christmas, Searl and Mrs. Fitzell had a falling out. Hoping for a reconciliation, he went to her second floor apartment on Christmas Eve, loaded with presents.

> I took all the presents to her and set them on the table. She threw them down the stairs after me. I was just totally crushed. I was an extraordinary person because of my ability to give, OK? I gave until I bled. I mean, when you tell your chick, "I know you like to go out and dance and drink. Listen, you go out with Joe Blow and I'll stay and watch the kids, and I'll be here when you get back." You know, how much more can you give? I gave so much I thought the little I was asking in return, there wasn't any way she couldn't give it. But she turned all that giving nature to remorse. All my dreams and hopes for family life were dashed—and that was all I wanted in this world.

After this rejection, he ran all over town spending money and cashing bad checks. His last purchase was a length of hose for a sprinkler system. With that in the car, he drove toward South Haven, stopping along the way to buy a gallon of A&W rootbeer and a big bag of nuts. Then, on a back road in the country near South Haven, he attached the hose to the exhaust pipe, put the other end through the window, and sat in the car eating nuts and drinking root beer, "having a big time leaving the world." He was just getting to the dizzy stage when a car stopped and the driver asked if he was all right. Searl said he was, and the man drove on. As the carbon monoxide began to work, he had the sensation that someone was pulling him down by the belt.

Shortly, the state police drove up, opened the door, and pulled him out of the fume-filled car. "It was obvious my intentions were serious. A couple of more minutes, the police said, would have done it." The police called Searl's mother and sister and took him to the state mental hospital in Kalamazoo. He spent two weeks there, getting, as he remembers it, little psychiatric attention. Someone took a short psychological profile, the chief psychiatrist spoke to him on a morning walk-through, but no one asked serious questions about the suicide attempt. "They might have recognized some signs I was ready to go off the deep end," Searl says. "It was a golden opportunity to nip me in the bud."

We have seen Searl casting about for a congenial form of heroism, a role worthy of his sense of his own importance. For a while on the Barrett's farm he was the hard worker, enjoying his solitude but also showing up his brother by getting up early and putting in a full day's work. Then, in junior high and high school, he was the "young hoodlum" extorting milk money, defying teachers, and finally stealing a car. When he first entered the army, he had a vision of himself as a paratrooper, probably as dramatic an assignment as any in the army. But shipping and receiving hardly answered his need. Refusing to be a clerk, he made himself a wild man, smashing windows to seize butcher knives and threatening murder in retaliation for the theft of a couple of bags of potato chips. Then he was the lover, giving incredibly of himself and, finally, when his gifts were rejected, arranging his own death.

Now, tragically, we see these last two roles combined. He is still the rejected lover moving toward death. At the same time, he is the outlaw, playing out a part he remembers from television or the movies:

> My plan all along, throughout the whole shoot-
> 'em-up time, was to die. Now with Betty I
> thought I had what I needed, and I did except for
> the fact that she wasn't—perhaps I didn't have
> what *she* needed. At any rate, she couldn't commit
> herself to me totally. Now, that was a case of, OK, I
> put all my eggs in one basket. This was *it*. Beyond
> this, there's nothing else. So when it fell through, I

just said, "This is the end of the world. There's nothing else for me in this world, so hell with it." But I felt the world owed me a last supper, and the last supper would be provided by—whoever I felt had enough money to provide my needs. So I would stick 'em up, get a couple of steaks, get a little beer, wine, whatever. I'd live fairly decent for three or four days and booze every night.

Searl himself cannot be sure how much deliberate intention there was in the murders. Sometimes it seems to him that he set out to commit a robbery and then went through the subsequent steps without conscious thought, as though he had been programmed.

I have to say I don't consciously remember ever sitting down and saying, "I am going to take this gun and go out and find this person and take this money and kill this person." There was never a plan, you know; it was a natural thing. It always seemed to me like I was an actor in a play that maybe I had seen on television or the movies or whatever. I acted the part of a robber. And a robber, once he has the money, then he ties the victims up, or pretends to do so, and at the first opportunity, pow. I didn't consciously decide I was going to do that; it was just something that was done.

At other times he is not sure that murder-without-intention sounds plausible:

Does it seem reasonable to you? I've always wondered, you know—a lot of people question whether that's possible. I just don't know how else it could be. Strange. You know what I'd like to do, I'd like to go back under hypnosis or some sort of a truth serum and see. 'Cause you know, it could be a fiction in my mind. It could be rationalization. Maybe it's buried so deeply that I just don't know.

It seems almost impossible that you could function from point A to point B without conscious thought. I know there was conscious thought, but I mean—to say, "Give me your money. Where is the back room?" And you say, "Back there." "Let's go." When we go back there, I say, "Turn around, hands behind you." And you say, "Ah, what are you going to do?" And I say, "Don't worry about it. I'm just going to tie you up." And you say, "OK." And you put your hands behind you, and I blow your brains out. It seems almost like that step, and this step, and that step all go together to lead up to that step. And you have to consciously consider. Now, like, tying up the hands was a subterfuge. All it was was a game of confidence, to put them at ease, to make the ultimate easier. But, you know, to do it without conscious thought is difficult to accept. To me it seems a little bit shaky. That would be something curious to find out, though. Maybe other people do the same thing, I don't know.

Probably not even hypnosis or truth serum would establish the degree of premeditation in those murders. But Searl's account makes clear the strange, apparently contradictory roles in which he cast himself. He was the rejected lover who gave of himself beyond anything that could be expected, who gave until he bled. "I was fully aware that I was giving that much. To have that misused was a mortal injury, and the world had done it." So he would leave the world, after a last supper. By a turn of logic, though, the body and the blood in this final sacrament would not be *his*, but those of a convenient garage attendant or school teacher. Not quite sure what part he was playing, perhaps, but convinced that his own death was not far off, he watched himself go through the steps that would lead to what the world owed him: a steak, a glass of wine, recognition of his superhuman stature.

(It may be that in discussing the murders, Searl adopts yet another role, not quite as dramatic as the earlier ones, but impressive in a way, nevertheless. Now he is the observer, looking at his former self with curiosity and detachment, trying to remember what he really felt, suspicious of rationalizations, judicious in his scientific interest.)

As for the murders themselves, the first occurred on April 6, 1964, in Battle Creek, Michigan, only twenty-five miles or so from Searl's home. Searl can't remember exactly what happened that day—in fact, in his confession he told the police that the killing took place in Paw Paw, west of Kalamazoo, instead of Battle Creek, to the east. No one was killed in Paw Paw, but Searl did correctly remember the victim, a twenty-three-year-old airman stationed at Fort Custer, who worked part-time at a gas station just off highway I-94. Searl stole about $150 from the station, took the man in the back room, and shot him. He remembers taking a "technical interest" in the killing, surprised, for example, "that the blood would shoot so far out of his head." Searl read in the newspaper later that the man was in a coma for twelve hours. Concerned that he might be suffering, Searl went to his mother's medical dictionary and looked up *coma*. He was relieved to find that one feels no pain in a coma; he was relieved again to read that the man had died.

"After that, I took a little more concern with where I shot. The next one I shot twice. It was his fault that I had to. He moved." This was another gas station attendant, a couple of weeks later. Searl hitch-hiked south to Lexington, Kentucky, then stole a car and drove to Manchester in the eastern Kentucky mountains. Again, he robbed a gas station and took the attendant into the back room. "He was a bouncy little guy—I suppose I chuckled at the time. He bounced a couple of feet in the air when I shot him." Searl seems to have taken a technical interest in this killing, too, and also a detached interest in his own psychology:

> The first shot ricocheted off the skull. It was supposed to be through the ear, but he turned his head just as I got ready to pull the trigger. And, you know, you go into a convulsion then. But his hand went back to his pocket. It's one of those things you catch out of the corner of your eye. At the time, I was involved in recocking the pistol—it was a double barrel. [Along the way he had traded the Bearcat for a Derringer.] But I remember that his hand went back. Then, you know, I shot him and killed him. But later, after they had me and I'd admitted to it, the cops came up from Kentucky and told me, "The guy had a .38." And I could have been dead. It's that simple. If this guy had— you know, that's how incredibly naive I was. There was no looking for any weapon or anything else. Maybe I was a naive kid, but it strikes me that I must have been following some prearranged, predetermined course that it just didn't enter my mind there could be a deviation from.

The third murder occurred near Death Valley, California, on May 23, 1964. Searl had been shooting signs and had one bullet left in the double-barrelled Derringer. Hitchhiking east from Los Angeles toward Las Vegas, he was picked up by a man in a station wagon, who asked Searl if he had a driver's license and then let him do the driving. The man kept protesting that he didn't have any money—which led Searl to think that he probably had a lot and that he ought to rob him. "Wasn't a very smart person, really. If he'd kept his mouth shut, I wouldn't even have thought about him." While they were riding in the car, Searl shot the man through the temple and kept on driving. For fifteen or twenty minutes he drove with the man slumped beside him, trying not to let the blood get on his white trench coat, before he found a turnoff and could dump the body on the desert. (The body was not found until November of 1966.) "I had a certain detachment, if you can visualize. There has to be some part of me left out."

That is the only time I have heard Searl concede that he might be missing some faculty that other people take for granted. On the whole he is well satisfied with his own composure, his lack of feeling. Here is his account of the last day and night of killing when he murdered Earl Foote, the school teacher, drove south to Indiana, robbed a gas station, and murdered the attendant. He felt little emotion about any of the people he killed, except for Foote:

> I was disgusted with him, disappointed, and probably a little bit angry—although less anger and more disappointment, disgust—because he didn't do what I told him to do. I told him, you know, "Don't make any noise and I won't hurt you." Now I don't know if that was true or not. But there was a possibility I might have let him go if he hadn't done anything, hadn't made any noise. Because I really didn't care that much, I didn't really consider being caught that much. It was kind of an alien thing, it didn't seem like something that could happen.
>
> Just, like, you know, following this night of Foote and the guy in Indiana, at about five, five-thirty in the morning, I raced Foote's car all the way from Elkhart to the Michigan line, racing with a guy in a Chevy, and we were hot-balling, you know, hundred-and-ten, we were topping them out all the way. And when I came on 131, they had a roadblock there, outside of Three Rivers, and it was specifically for me, for the stickup that I had pulled. But I come round that big curve outside of Three Rivers, and as soon as I clear the curve and straighten back out, there's the roadblock. Now it was really too late to evade the roadblock without

being conspicuous, but I just drive right straight up to it, roll the window down as I come easing to the stop, and say, "Yeah, what's the trouble, Officer?" And the sergeant on the roadblock says, "A little armed robbery. OK. Go ahead." Now I got Foote in the trunk, blood all over the bumper, the car was literally in shambles—I slept in it. You know these are trained law-enforcement personnel, and I was so cool that, you know, no problem, go ahead. He didn't ask for an ID or registration or anything.

They'd of had me right there. You know, everything would have been over right at that point, if I hadn't projected some image of coolness or invulnerability or whatever. But I just didn't consider it a feasible thing that I could be caught. I don't know, state of mind I guess. But I didn't do things to evade capture, as such. I just did whatever was called for. You just don't sleep in a car with a stiff all night long if you're worried about being caught.

9.

Reflections on Murder

Searl is not fully aware, I think, of his need to cast himself in some heroic role and of the incongruity between the roles he chooses. In his mind, it seems natural that the devoted lover, capable of giving until he bled, should be transformed in a matter of weeks to the murderer so self-possessed that he is passed without question through the road block set up expressly for him, so contemptuous of capture that he sleeps in the car with the body of a man he has just killed. But he has thought about the murders in the leisure of fourteen years in prison and has sorted out his own feelings about them. He states his conclusions with the conviction of one who has been over the arguments thoroughly in his mind, and sometimes he speaks with a preacherly cadence:

> If you eliminate the life, there is no remorse, on their part. If I kill you right now, you will not regret it. You will not regret not seeing your wife, or your kids, or not being with them. You won't regret it, because you'll never know it. [That's true, but . . .] It's very true, and there's no *but* to it. It will hurt *them*, and that's my problem today. It's

91

precisely what I was saying when I said *guilt*. I don't guilt for the person who's dead, because it would be irrelevant. There's nothing to guilt for him about, because he doesn't know anything, doesn't feel anything. I didn't take anything away from him because you can't take what one never had. [You took the other half of his life.] He can't miss what he's never had. It's the end of pain and misery.

The only thing that I'm concerned about—and you can call it gross, or you can call it cold, or unfeeling, or whatever—but the only thing I care about is that woman and those kids, who I deprived of a father and a husband. OK? I'm guilty about that, I grieve about that. But I don't grieve about the individual, because he's gone. Who knows, I don't know whether I did him a favor or not. At the very least, I didn't hurt him. I never hurt anybody—willingly. I'm talking about those whom I shot. I was very careful to kill and not maim. Maybe that's a rationalization, maybe it's a justification, but I don't feel that it is. I think it's not good, but on the other hand, it's somehow acceptable in a sense. In other words, I'm not a barbarian, not a fiend; I am not a cruel and heartless person. I did what I felt I had to do, in a compassionate way. Now I could have been another Tommy. I could have put plastic bags over people's heads and suffocated them and all that kind of sick shit. I could have stabbed them to death, which is horrifying. That's sickness, to me. That's degenerate.

Searl has the murders and their consequences all worked out in his mind. He feels guilt for the pain and loss he has caused the family of the dead man but not for the death itself, since the dead cannot suffer. The murders, though not good, were executed cleanly, with as little pain as possible, and they are "somehow acceptable." On hearing this reasoning, my first impulse, as the brackets indicate, was to argue. But it seems more useful, on second thought, to look at Searl's reasoning as an extreme and therefore vivid paradigm of the process all of us must go through in coming to an understanding with the world.

If Ernest Becker is right in his restatement of the world-view arrived at by Existentialists such as Kierkegaard and post-Freudian psychologists such as Otto Rank, man's dilemma is profound and unavoidable. Unlike the other animals who do what they do instinctively, man is self-conscious. This means, on one hand, that each person believes himself to be uniquely important, worthy of immortality. Though he sees other people dying and is able to understand, rationally, that he must die, still underneath that rational acceptance, he does not really believe in his own death. In a sense, the world exists because he perceives it, and it is inconceivable that it could exist with that perceiver gone.

On the other hand, each person is constantly reminded of his body's grossness and frailty. He may feel himself to be an expansive spirit, important to the cosmos, but he can't help noticing that in fact he is made of decaying flesh. The world is far more awesome and complex and terrible than anything he could conceive, and in a remarkably short time it will dispense with him and go its own enormous way without so much as a backward glance. Of all the animals, only man has the burden of knowing this, of living his life in the presence of death.

According to Rank and Becker, much of human psychology, normal and abnormal, may be seen as a way of coping with this dilemma. Among more specific devices, we all undertake to put from our minds the real terror of our situation by creating fictions of two kinds: first, we make ourselves "heroes," worthy of cosmic recognition; second, we attempt to tame the world by shrinking it to what we imagine we can comprehend and control. As we have already seen, Ralph Searl's behavior, however erratic it may seem, is consistent at least in its pursuit of the heroic. He seems determined that his life, both in the acting and in the telling of it, should be spectacular. And at least in the episodes we have seen so far, it must be spectacular in the short run. He has shown little patience in *preparing* himself for a heroism that will emerge later on. Right now, he must prove himself superior to his brother if it means threatening to kill him with a pistol. Right now, he must have the respect of the other men in the army barracks if it means stealing butcher knives and running berserk through the compound. Right now, he must win the woman and establish himself as head of the family, or he will commit suicide—or murder.

Now, in his reflections on murder, we see the universal dilemma unfold itself with a vividness that fortunately we do not often encounter. He comes to the heart of the matter immediately by asserting that he feels no guilt for the death itself. The murdered man can feel no regret, can feel nothing. He cannot miss what he has never had, so remorse for him would be irrelevant. In fact, this argument does state with cruel directness half of the truth about our life in the world: we die and are done with it. We know nothing, feel nothing. We have no part in whatever happens afterward.

This is the fact that, according to Kierkegaard, lies behind our fear and trembling. But notice that Searl manages to eliminate any sense of dread; that is what makes his statement so chilling. The dead are dead, he says, as if that fact called for no feeling. Then, he reveals the turns of thought he has used to skirt around the dread of death. There are three of these. First, he thinks, as we all tend to do, of *someone else's* death: the deaths of the men he killed, or hypothetically my death, if he were to kill me. Viewed strictly from the outside, the finality of death is obvious and indisputable. It requires no particular emotion.

Second, he focuses his attention and his sense of responsibility on the survivors, the wife and children of the dead man. This is reasonable, of course; we all tend to make death manageable by thinking about the familiar, perhaps soluble problems of those who are still living. We bring in hot meals or offer to look after the children. This is particularly convenient for a murderer. If he thinks only about the loss suffered by the wife and children of the murdered man, his responsibility diminishes with time.

> Now I can say I feel for that woman and those kids, and I really do, I honestly do, but I know that she went out west and got married again, and she's married, as far as I know, today. Those kids have a father. And I hope to God that she made the right choice and they have the right father. OK? So I don't feel that strong a guilt, in this particular case. She has remedied it the best way she could. I hope she made a good choice. If she didn't, I can't be responsible for that. 'Cause it's got to end somewhere, OK?

As the survivors make their own choices and rebuild their lives, Searl's responsibility becomes less and less—whereas if he were to allow himself to think about the world from the point of view of the murdered men themselves, the loss would be absolute and irreparable. If he were guilty at the moment he fired the gun, he would remain equally guilty the rest of his life.

A third way of separating murder from the sense of terror or awe that we feel at our own oncoming deaths is to concentrate on circumstantial details rather than the thing itself. If death is inflicted cleanly, painlessly, then it is "acceptable," whereas murder by suffocation or stabbing, with the grisly paraphernalia of knives and plastic bags, is horrifying. When a friend dies in an accident, we want to know just where it happened, and how, and at what time—information that, even as we are asking, we know to be of trivial importance. Following this familiar habit of thought, Searl has transferred the horror of death to the *process* of killing and in that way has exonerated himself from some of the burden of murder. This allows him, too, a final superiority over his brother. In his murders, he carefully avoided inflicting pain—he even "made the ultimate easier" by letting his victims believe they were just going to have their hands tied—whereas his brother, not fastidious about method, brought death in a more horrible form. By attending strictly to the process, Searl can almost make it sound as though his brother was a murderer while he himself was a surgeon or a dentist, doing what had to be done as painlessly as possible.

Here is Searl, discussing free choice, alternatives, and the acceptance of punishment:

> I did what I had to do. Have you ever done what you had to do? Do you suppose we have a choice, in life? [Yes, I think we do.] Ah, but at what point? At what point do we have choice in life? We have a choice only when we become so aware of self and all the contributing factors—then, that's the only time we're armed with the ability to deal with life on *our* terms, to make the changes, make correct decisions and so forth. I never reached that point till I was probably twenty-five years old. Like I said, whichever way the wind blew, that's the way I went.
>
> Now I don't justify any actions based on that. I believe that I'm guilty, I believe that I'm in the right place, for what I did. I should be dead. You should have killed me a long time ago, you really should have. And that's exactly what I told them when they busted me: "Send me to Indiana where they've got the death penalty." That's all you can do for me. But society has chosen to confine me, in this particular situation, and consequently they will reap the rewards of that. OK? On a day-to-day level, I'm in the right place, and all I say is, Don't fuck with me, because you've waited too long to do that. If you wanted to fuck with me, you should

have did it with that electric switch way back when, not now. I'm beyond that point.

Searl introduces a rather sophisticated notion of free will here: that choice depends on self-awareness, on the ability to sort out alternatives in the external world and to identify and deal with internal compulsions that may drive one toward a certain course of action. (He develops these ideas more fully later on.) But he does not argue that his lack of awareness at age nineteen frees him from responsibility for the murders. "On a day-to-day level," he acknowledges that justice has been done and that he deserves the punishment he is receiving. His heroism now, in prison, consists in accepting punishment without complaint, without whining or making excuses. He will take the full measure of suffering— more than he inflicted on others, in his weighing of the matter. He is in the right place.

Further, in Searl's view, his suffering justifies a certain status, a degree of dignity, in prison itself. Since society chose not to kill him at the time of the murders—possibly lacking the courage or directness that he himself possessed—he does not want anyone "fucking with him" now. He is offering a strong man's bargain to his keepers: I'll accept imprisonment stoically, without complaint. But don't mistake me for an ordinary prisoner. There is a grandeur to my suffering as there was an inhuman calm to my murders. Don't think I am going to take on guilts that are not mine, and don't think I will tolerate any stupid or brutal treatment. You are dealing with someone formidable. The reflections continue:

> What can I say about the past? I can say, damn, I wish somebody had made me wiser. I wish somebody had taught me, years and years before this ever happened, that there is a choice in life. That you don't act because it seems right or feels right or it's the only thing you can do. When I had everything taken from me that was important to me, I struck out at the world and I drew blood. I

97

made them pay. Why did I do that? Because I had no alternative.

On a day-to-day level, yes, I am guilty; on a philosophical level, I am not responsible. I am a creature of my environment. The influences on me made me what I am. I am no more responsible for that than I am for the sun shining. It's the way things are. You were given a set of alternatives in life. Now apparently your alternatives were of such a variety—or contained enough truths—to be viable to every situation you've encountered. OK? Or you have backup alternatives, or whatever. You've been able to cope and deal with what you've come up against. I wasn't given the alternatives that you were. This is an obvious fact of life, because if I had been I would have chosen different alternatives.

I have reached a level of self-awareness where I'm now capable of making choices on a reasonably free basis, OK? You know, the thing I now believe is that I can take the impulse to kick that chair and go back to point x, y, or z and say, OK, I saw someone kick a chair like that to express deep anger or hate or resentment or whatever, and I'm mimicking that act. Consequently I can say, hey, that's not a good idea to kick that chair—and stop that particular habit. But it's all a matter of habits. You either accept the habits as being viable or you don't and you change them. That's the only thing that free will has to do with it.

I know Sarah Barrett tried to commit suicide when she was like twelve, thirteen—you know, lost love, the end of the world. She took a whole bottle of aspirins. At that point in life she was my sister, quasi-mother, companion, friend, anything. When she did that, it impressed the hell out of me. You know, that's where you go when you get that low. I knew how she felt about her boyfriend who had jilted her, and consequently when I entered into that same set of circumstances, that was my alternative. And someone allowed me to go on believing that was a damn good way to go. So I said, OK, this is what's got to be done. But somehow someone instilled in me the idea that you were *owed* some form of happiness in life. A degree of happiness.

Were you asked to be brought on this earth? No, you had no alternative, no choice in it, but you're here because someone else decided it. Well, that someone else owes you something, then. You know, mother and father is world. So if mom and dad owe you something, the world owes you something. So then when you've done the best you can with what you've got, and I feel I did the best I could—I gave all I could and it wasn't enough. If I'm this gross a failure that I can give every last ounce of me and it can be thrown aside like last week's garbage, where do I go from here? The only alternative is to leave this world. The world owes me something, a moment of pleasure at least. Once you give it to me, I'll let it go, and you can all go to hell, with me or without me, I don't care which, but I'm going.

Here Searl talks about responsibility and choice in quite a careful and consistent way. He allows for a modicum of free choice at any stage in anyone's life, but only choice among the alternatives that parents or past experience have provided. In some cases (his own), this may amount to no choice at all. None of the alternatives that "feel right" or seem inevitable is in fact adequate to cope with the urgencies of one's life. With greater self-awareness, Searl argues, it is possible to enlarge one's choices or to follow back one alternative to its source and discard it if it promises to be a fruitless piece of mimicry. This is a defensible view, I believe, psychologically and philosophically. It is also a view that allows Searl the heroic dignity he has needed all along. He does not have to see himself, at present, as a product only of his environment, blown by the winds of circumstance. He believes he has now achieved a self-awareness that allows him to choose among a wider range of alternatives—in short, to act freely. But this view of free will also provides an explanation for his murders: then, at nineteen, he had not really become free. In a practical way, he takes responsibility for his actions, yet, taking a larger view, he does not hold himself responsible. His environment provided the choices he had to work with—none of them, he believes, adequate to his situation. So he is suffering, without complaint, for the failings of his parents and other adults. In a sense, he has taken upon himself the sins of the world.

To bring the argument full circle, Searl expresses transparently, vividly, and with characteristic self-dramatization a partial truth that we all must acknowledge finally: we are gross failures. We give all we can and it is not enough. We are thrown aside like last week's garbage. That is to say, no matter how much we make of our lives, no matter how faithfully we work and love, still we die and the world goes on without us.

I am not saying, of course, that Searl's rejection by Betty Fitzell was a legitimate cause for desperation or an excuse for murder. People are rejected by their lovers every day and their lives go on without violence. All I am saying is that this situation, as Searl has dramatized it, will serve very well as a representation in miniature of the situation of man in the world. "Last week's garbage" is accurate enough. It is man's characteristic misery that he knows and resents it. According to Becker, every person feels that the world *owes* him something, and not just a steak and a glass of wine. We feel we are owed "cosmic specialness;" each person must "justify himself as an object of primary value in the universe." He must be a hero. "If everyone honestly admitted his urge to be a hero it would be a devastating release of truth." (Becker, 5)

Searl's life may interest us because of the utter transparency of his demand for heroism, the blatancy, crudeness, violence, and persistence with which he insists that the world give him his due. Here the universal need for recognition and admiration is projected starkly against the backdrop of death. Becker writes:

> To become conscious of what one is doing to earn his feeling of heroism is the main self-analytic problem of life. Everything painful and sobering in what psychoanalytic genius and religious genius have discovered about man revolves around the terror of admitting what one is doing to earn his self-esteem. This is why human heroics is a blind drivenness that burns people up: in passionate people, a screaming for glory as uncritical and reflexive as the howling of a dog. In the more passive masses of mediocre men it is disguised as they humbly and complainingly follow out the roles that society provides for their heroics and try to earn their promotions within the system. (Becker, 6)

Searl's history must be the classic example of a "screaming for glory as uncritical and reflexive as the howling of a dog." In fact, I suspect Becker had not encountered quite so pure an example of his passionate man when he wrote the passage above. If he had, he might have spoken less condescendingly of the more modest forms of heroism that ordinary people pursue. He acknowledges that if everyone were to express openly the drive for heroism that is the tacit project of his life, it would release such pent-up force that societies might well be destroyed. Searl's life is a perfect illustration of that point.

101

10.

Mike and the Chimpanzee

Ralph Searl tends to place part of the blame for his murders on the victims themselves. If the man in California had not protested so much, had not kept talking about how little money he had, Searl wouldn't have thought anything about him. Or if the school teacher had not pounded on the roof of the trunk, he might not have killed him. In his mind, one incident lends credibility to the conjecture that some of his victims might have saved themselves if they had behaved differently: one person who might have been a victim escaped alive and well. Between the murder of the California man and the murder of the school teacher, Searl was picked up, hitch-hiking, by Mike, the only man for whom I have heard him express unqualified admiration. Here is Searl's account of the three days he spent in Mike's truck travelling from Nevada to South Haven, Michigan (an account confirmed, in its outlines, by Mike himself in a telephone conversation with the Kalamazoo *Gazette* shortly after the events took place). Among other things, it provides an instance of the strange relationship that may develop between a criminal and his victim:

It's about eight o'clock, almost dark, when Mike picks me up with the chimpanzee. What it was, he had a Chevy panel truck, the back was almost all caged, and Zippy the ice-skating chimpanzee was in there. You ever see him on Ed Sullivan? I had, way back when he was *the* ice-skating chimpanzee, the only one they had. I get in and there's this ungodly howling and screeching and I'm looking through the back window and, what? a chimpanzee? What kind of people is this? Mike was decent people. He was turned off on life, I know that. I think he'd been divorced. Anyway, he runs down his history: he'd just completed a European tour with the Ice-Capades and was on his way back to Chicago. We're travelling along and right away I get to thinking, Mmmm, probably got some money. Well, we'd better stick him up.

That night he slept in a motel and I slept in the front of the truck. We took off the next day and drove and got to know each other real well. So that night it was raining and dark and it was about, I don't know, ten or ten-thirty or so. There was a big river coming up on the map and I decided, OK, right here, that's it. We were close to a town, close enough there were street lights over the highway. So I hold the pistol, it was a chrome-plated Derringer. I'm setting here in the truck and he is driving and I'm waiting for him to see it. And he don't see it . . . and he don't see it . . . and he don't see it. "Mike? Do you see what I got in my hand?"

"No, it's too dark." Then the street light comes up and he sees it. "Huh? What you gonna do with that?"

"It's a stickup, Mike. I'm gonna stick you up."

"But you don't need that."

"Well, give me your wallet, Mike. Give it to me. Give me your ring, Mike. Yeah, it's beautiful." A blue star sapphire with diamonds in it. He was kind of reluctant on that. "Errrumm." Finally he takes it off and gives it to me.

"Pull down the next side street. OK now, let's go to the back of the truck." We go back and he opens up the panel truck. I tell him, "Open up the chimp cage," and he opens that up. The chimp jumps out right away, arms all around his neck, looking over at me just like a little kid. So he's calming the chimp down, "Relax, everything's OK."

"Get in the cage, Mike."

"Come on, you got to be kidding."

"No, in the cage, Mike."

"All right, all right, all right." He gets in the cage and I lock him in, and I take off, driving the truck. You know I put Mike in the cage with the chimp and I was just going to slide the whole mess off in the river. I actually looked for the river.

He waits about five minutes. "Ralph, you gotta let me out of here. It stinks." It stunk something ferocious in that chimp cage. So I ignore him. "Come on, I won't give you no trouble. I swear. Give you my word, I won't give you no problems. Just let me out of here. It's killing me."

I like the guy. So I say, "All right, I'm gonna let you out. You're gonna give me no problems. You don't say nothing."

"Don't worry about it. No problems." So I pull over and let him out. That's when I stopped looking for the river. Along about eleven-thirty or so, something like that, we run low on gas and we need something to eat. I got all the money and I bring it with me. "Look, Mike, give me your word you won't say nothing to nobody, no signs, nothing."

"Don't worry about it."

"All right, OK, Mike." We pull in this combination gas pump and a little restaurant and I tell the guy to fill it up, check the oil, and all that. We go on in and sit down, and she comes over, the broad who is running this restaurant, and we order

105

eggs and potatoes, scrambled eggs and hash potatoes, toast, milk, and coffee. Mike gets the same thing. We're sitting there waiting for the order to come. She's brought the coffee, so we're sitting there, mixing it up—he's looking at her. He's, you know, he's getting ready to—I say, "Mike."

"Mmm, I'm sorry." He starts stirring his coffee. "You know, Ralph, I don't care about the money. The only thing that really bothers me is the ring. My mother gave that to me on my last birthday, and there's no way it can be replaced. Sentimental value and all that. The money I can probably—well, I think it's on the insurance or something. But even if they could replace the ring, it wouldn't be the same." So I'm looking at it, and it *is* a beautiful ring. I love that son of a bitch. But I felt like dirt right then, and I gave it to him.

"God," he says, "there's nothing I can say. Thanks." So we go ahead and eat.

He's so, he's so *good* that I just decided to trust him. When I finished eating I threw a five on the table to pay for it. I've got to use the bathroom, so I go and use the bathroom in the other end of the building in the gas station part. I come out of the bathroom—I stole a radio out of there, a transistor—I come out of there and Mike is sitting in the truck, the motor running. I'd left the keys in there to let the gas station guys work on it. He's sitting there and got the truck running. Quite a guy. I look at him and I just smile. What can I say?

We take off again and he's driving now and long about one, one-thirty I start getting tired so I say, "Look, I got to get some sleep."

And he says, "Go ahead."

"Look, Mike, you promised no hassle, no problems, right?"

"Promised."

Mike and the Chimpanzee

"OK." I decided I had to trust him completely. I take the pistol out and I hold it like this. He finally sees it and he holds his hand underneath it and I drop the pistol in his hand.

"What do you want me to do with this?"

"What do you want to do with it?"

"I don't even want to touch it." He hands it back. OK, cool. I put it in the pocket of my topcoat and lay the coat on the back of the seat next to me. Then I turn over and go to sleep against the door.

I wake up and we're in the middle of some town—I think it was in Missouri or some damn place—and we're right in the middle of the town, stopped at a red light. The clock said it was about eight, eight-fifteen. The first thing I do is I come around and hit the coat. No gun. "Hey, what did you do with the gun?"

"I threw it in the river."

"You didn't do that! You son of a bitch, now I got no gun. How could you do that to me? I told you there's nothing to worry about, I'm not going to hurt you!"

"It made me nervous. I got a nervous stomach and I was upset. I had to do it."

"Dumb fucker." I'm hot. I'm mad. Threw my gun away. I'm really pissed.

That day we got to Chicago. I ain't got no gun. I'm paying the way, though, with his money. When we get to Chicago, he says, "Where do you want to go? Where do you want me to let you off?" You know how the freeways are around Chicago, it's a bitch to get a ride out.

"You're going to Michigan, aren't you?" he says. "Look, I'll take you to South Haven and drop you off there and I can just drive back to Chicago. That way you'll be up off the freeways." You know, cool, cool. So he takes me to South Haven. I don't know if he'd ever been there or not, but he pulls up right behind a State Police post. He stops the truck.

"You son of a bitch, you're gonna make sure I'm not gonna hurt you. You pull right up behind the cops."

He says, "No, you know." So we go back and we start getting the suitcases out. He gets out his two, and he puts them on the ground. I had been telling him he dressed like something out of *Esquire*, mohairs and all this. That was back in semi-Nehru times, you know, when the Nehru jackets and all that were popular. He starts opening his suitcases and he says, "OK, that's for you and that's for me." He actually divided everything he had right in two. Gave me half and he kept half. All these thick, heavy mohairs from England and all over the damn place. They were just phenomenal. So I'm really messed up. I'm dumbfounded. Wow. This is too much.

So I packed everything back up in my suitcase and he packed his back up. He puts them in the trunk and he reaches in by the wheel-well, by the cage, and he comes up and turns around and he holds his hand out. He drops the pistol back in my hand. "You son of a bitch, I thought you threw it in the river."

"I just—it made me nervous. I had to get it out of the way. You know I wouldn't do that. You know I wouldn't throw your stuff away."

Then we get ready to part company, and he hesitates for a minute and just kind of stands there. I start to walk away. He says, "I hate to ask but I don't have any money to get back to Chicago."

"How much do you need?"

"Food for me, food for the chimp, gas, about forty dollars."

So I give him forty dollars and I tell him, "I want you to do me a favor, Mike. I don't want you to turn this in until two weeks from today. Can you do that?"

"Well, it's going to hurt my insurance claim. All right, I won't turn it in for two weeks." Actually, he waited a lot longer than that. Let me think of the time sequences here. After he left, there was a couple of days, so we're talking roughly two weeks until I got busted. Then I was in County Jail for at least a month, maybe even two months before he ever turned it in. He waited that long. He must never have turned it in to the insurance company.

I always wanted to write him, you know in later years. "What did you actually think . . . what could have been in your mind when you handed the pistol back. Or when you were sitting there with the truck running when I came out of the bathroom. You could have been gone, you know there was nothing to stop you." It was purely that he decided I could trust him and he had so much class, so much honor about himself that he performed in that way. That's an extraordinary person. Could you envision yourself doing it? Even if you said, "Hey, don't worry. I'm not going to do a thing wrong"? Once the guy's out of sight with the gun, what the hell? Everybody for themselves. But he wouldn't do it. He's that kind of a person. That's an extraordinary person. You know I don't have his address, all I have is his name. But I know I could contact him through the Ice-Capades or whatever and strike it up. But I don't know. I guess I may be afraid of the answer. I'd rather cherish the thought of it.

My first impression, hearing this story, was that there was not one madman in that truck but two. After all, it was that pistol, which Mike so honorably returned to Ralph, that killed two men a couple of weeks later. But there is a ritual quality about this three-day journey, as well. Once Ralph let Mike out of the cage, each was in the other's power; each had the means to inflict death or imprisonment on the other. Cautiously, they performed a kind of dance, circling around each other, making gestures of trust and generosity as though they were friends. In mutual danger, they each depended on the self control, the good manners of the other. By the time they got to South Haven, they had survived three days together and apparently felt an attachment, even gratitude to each other. We may be tempted to see Mike as something close to an accomplice in crime, but we should not forget that the people who picked Searl up just before and just after Mike did, came out of the experience dead. However it may look at this distance, Mike and Zippy managed to execute a careful figure eight on thin ice.

It is clear how much pleasure Searl takes in this incident, and it is not hard to discover why. Certainly, he admires Mike's coolness, his presence of mind, his ability to improvise—qualities that Searl admires in himself as well. More than that, without committing any violence, Searl found that he inspired a kind of loyalty in Mike, something like friendship. Even when the gun was not in Searl's possession, Mike shared his clothes with him, treated him with deference. In the midst of his murders, here was power of a subtler and more satisfying sort.

11.

Prison: Marquette

After a three-day ride with Mike and the chimpanzee, after shooting Earl Foote in the trunk of his own car, after taking the Elkhart gas station attendant to the men's room and shooting him, after racing north again before dawn and being waved through the roadblock set up to stop him, Ralph Searl turned off of Highway 131 at the Stadium Drive exit in Kalamazoo—and the car broke down. He abandoned it by the side of the road, with Foote's body still in the trunk, and hitch-hiked into town. Later in the day, a state trooper saw blood stains on the rear bumper of the abandoned car and had it towed to the State Police post at Paw Paw, where the trunk was forced open.

For the next few days, the Kalamazoo *Gazette* carried stories about the victim and his family, speculation about possible links between this murder and the one in Elkhart, and some technical discussion about whether he had been shot before or after he was put in the trunk of the car. There were some finger prints, but in truth the police had little to go on.

Six days after the murder, talking in the evening with Betty Fitzell and a friend, Edmund Scott, at an apartment house on Cobb Street, Searl mentioned that he had killed some people. He said he intended to talk to a priest and then commit suicide. When he could, Scott left the room and called the police—just before midnight on June 4, 1964. Two officers came to the address Scott gave them, parked a short distance away, and walked to the house. Scott met them outside the house, and while they were talking, Searl walked out. According to the *Gazette*, one of the officers called out, "Are you Ralph Searl?" Searl answered yes. The police asked if he had a gun. Searl told them which pocket it was in. One policeman asked, "Did you kill Foote?" Searl said, "That school teacher? Yes, I did." At the police station, he confessed to all five murders and was arraigned later that night.

Searl was expertly defended by Eugene Field, his court-appointed attorney (who refused to accept payment from the County for his services), but the jury was not persuaded by the argument that Searl was temporarily insane at the time of the murders. They found him guilty of first-degree murder, and Judge Raymond Fox sentenced him to life in prison without the possibility of parole. Michigan law makes that sentence mandatory.

He was sent first to the state prison at Jackson and after six months transferred to Marquette in the Upper Peninsula. He stayed there for seven years until, in 1972, the Michigan Supreme Court remanded his case to the Circuit Court in Kalamazoo for retrial. For Searl, these seven years were as intense, perhaps, as the ones that preceded them. He was still aggressive, violent, and demanding. The Deputy Warden at Marquette remembers him as a dangerous man, one who took advantage of his murders to impress other inmates—and guards as well. But now, instead of ranging from Michigan to Mexico, his world had shrunk to a prison, or a single cell.

In reflecting on his murders, Karamazov said that he was twenty-five years old before he had enough self-awareness to make deliberate choices, to deal with life on his own terms. Before that, "whichever way the wind blew, that's the way I went." His twenty-fifth birthday came toward the end of his stay in Marquette, and much of what happened there may be seen as a characteristically fierce attempt to define himself against the rigid patterns of the prison world.

Marquette, though it is still in Michigan, is almost five hundred miles from Kalamazoo, further away than Louisville, Kentucky, or Rochester, New York. So being sent there, Searl was a long way from family and friends. But he intensified his isolation in two ways. First, during much of the seven years in Marquette, he refused mail and visits from his family. In speaking about this, he sounded, at first, as though it was simply a matter of indifference—his family was not important to him: "I just made up my mind, you know. That's the lack of emotion I have, for the family. It was *easy* for me. I said I don't want anything to do with them and that's it."

But as he talked further, it became clear that it was not just indifference. Prison officials apparently had held up both incoming and outgoing mail sometimes during the six months that he was in Jackson, and he was disappointed and angry that his mother and sister were not aggressive enough to do something about it:

> I was hurt, you know. What it was, Mom had come up with Leslie and set down to visit, and the first thing they come in, "How come you haven't been writing?"
>
> "I have been, how come you haven't been?"
>
> "Well, we have, too."
>
> "Well, OK, it's quite obvious what's happening is that the officials are holding it up."
>
> "They wouldn't do *that*."
>
> I say, "*Come on*, they're holding up the mail. Now, what are you going to do about it?"
>
> "Oh, what could we do?" you know, and they're all off like that. I explained to them exactly how to go about it, right down to filing a suit. "We'll take care of it." They left. I set there for two

more weeks. I don't get letter one, I don't get no word from them whatsoever.

Here, one can see a characteristic mixture of feelings on Searl's part: anger at his mother and sister for not doing what he tells them; a certain indifference, a confidence that he can get along without them if need be; and, at the same time, a real desire for mail. Further, we can see, back here at the beginning of his prison career, an awareness that prison staff members do things for reasons and that those reasons can be understood and used, an awareness that if he puts his mind to it he can have considerable control over the way he is treated in prison.

This is not the end of the mail story. "What I ended up doing, I ended up threatening the deputy." After a visit by Julie and his younger sister Sally, he was taken back to his cell.

Twenty minutes later, I'm setting in this cell, there were six mattresses in there—I mean they really jammed us—nothing, you couldn't smoke, no nothing. I was setting in this damn cell, here comes this deputy, assistant deputy warden, up to my bars with mail like this in his arms. Twenty-eight pieces of mail, from Gene and everybody. [Eugene Field, his attorney.] You know the first question he asked me? "What happened? How come you didn't get your mail?" I said, "You son of a bitch. If I ever catch you, I'll kill you." That was the end of that. You don't play that in prison. You don't threaten deputies. I mean the gall of this son of a bitch to ask me a question like that. What happened? Like I'm supposed to know what happened to my mail. He's got it all in his arms.

Oh, was I hot.

At any rate, when he left Jackson for Marquette, he left his family and the mail behind. "When they put me on the bus to Marquette, I made up my mind. I said, OK, I've got enough aggravations the way things are, I don't need any more. It's quite obvious that all they're going to do is give me aggravations, so I said to hell with it. I'll go for myself and they [his family] can go for themselves. Really, it works kind of good in a way."

So the first way in which Searl intensified his isolation at Marquette was by cutting himself off from his family and friends. The second was more drastic: of his seven years at Marquette, he spent approximately two years in the hole, in solitary or semisolitary confinement. In prison, a serious violation of the rules is punished by "segregation"; the prisoner is moved from the general population, where he can enjoy considerable freedom of movement, to a special cell block called the hole, a prison within the prison. There he finds little or no recreation, poor food, and in extreme cases almost no contact with other prisoners. On a couple of occasions Searl deliberately set out to have himself sent to the hole, but usually he just acted the way he acted and didn't mind if he was sent to the hole as a consequence. In retrospect, though, even his recklessness seems intentional, as though he were looking for a way to withdraw or test himself.

What does one *do* for weeks or months in a solitary cell? Writers write, sometimes, and readers read. Ever since the third-grade birdhouse, Searl had been good at making things. In the hole, he made things out of whatever materials he could find. Among other things, he improvised a wheel-shaped contraption in which he could watch spiders devour flies. The spokes were twelve small tunnels made by wrapping the clear plastic from pouches of Chippewa tobacco around a pencil and melting the edges together, forming twelve fat, transparent straws. At the end of each one was a small house made from a cardboard cigarette pack. At the hub was a round control center made out of clear plastic with a medicine cup in the top as a cap. (Searl called it the control center matter-of-factly. In a prison, the control center is the main desk, usually in the middle of the complex of build-

115

ings, where orders are issued and bells are rung, where prisoners go for permission to pass to another area, etc.)

Now out of this control center, there's tubes coming to each one of these packs. And up at the front of each tube, at the control center, there's a little gate. Little cardboard gate. Now I got twelve spiders that I caught. I'd lay there with a towel, you know. I'd see one go past on the rock, I'd throw the towel out there and lay there for literally hours on end. And when he'd come back by, as soon as he got on the towel, I'd jerk him in the cell. Then I got him, he's mine. Boom. Put him in his pack.

Then I'd spend hours on end hitting flies. I got a rubber band, you know a real thin one? Broke it in two. Then I take syrup or something off the breakfast, put it on a little spot on the ceiling or floor, you know, where the sunlight's at, and when a fly come up there, I'd try to hit him—just stun him. Half of them you kill but every once in a while you stun one just enough to grab him, drop him in the control center. Whichever spider I want to feed, I open his gate, leave the rest of them closed, and the fly eventually goes down in there.

The spider's all poised when he hears him coming down the tube—you know, the fly's buzzing up against the plastic trying to get back out once I closed the gate on him. Then you lay there for an hour or so and watch that fly work its way down, and all of a sudden it discovers that there's a spider in there and it tries to get back out. The spider's not going for it. It chases it up the thing, grabs it and drags it back down in. Then, you know, you get as close as you can and try to watch him as his little pinchers go at him. So I spent eight months, keeping twelve spiders alive. And I didn't want to come out of there.

To me, hearing about it at a distance of some fifteen years, Searl's time in Marquette seems odd and contradictory. Even his account of the spider-and-fly machine shows mixed feelings: pride in the construction of the thing, the craftsmanship; pride in the patience needed to capture the spiders and flies; pleasure in his ability to manage the creation he looked down on, to predict what would happen and watch his predictions come true; and more grisly pleasure in seeing the flies' panic and the spiders' pincers going to work. He was the artificer, constructing a small labyrinth of plastic and paper in order to dominate the days and months of solitude, constructing a tiny prison in which he opened one gate to each stunned fly and closed it behind. It was a small, carefully-made world whose principles were *devour* and *control*.

As Karamazov talks about the time spent in Marquette's segregation blocks, the severest punishment the Michigan penal system can inflict, he shows no signs of self pity. He considers it a good thing, a chance to come to some sort of understanding with himself:

> Those things, they *sound* extraordinary or something. Like two years in the hole, you know, that sounds extraordinary to people, but once you're into it, it actually becomes enjoyable—if you like yourself or, you know, if you're capable of liking yourself. That's where I learned to like myself. I always hated myself before then, but I started making—you know, OK, this is what I'm going to do if I ever get out. I'm going to do this and that. I got into that positive thinking, or style of thought. It made a big change in my life. I wouldn't trade it for anything in the world. It was the best experience I ever had, so far as changing myself. I'd recommend it for everybody. When you get eighteen, you go to the hole for two years and then . . . [We laugh.] It definitely has advantages, though.

It was during his stay in Marquette, particularly in seg-regation, that he went into his own mind and "isolated the negatives there and expunged them." That is, he figured out exactly what he didn't like about himself and planned to change it. He hated his name, first of all. In the neighbor-hood on East Main Street, everybody knew those damn Searl boys. Now he shrivelled inside everytime he heard the word "Searl"—and in prison he was always called by his last name. He hated his ears that stuck out, and his chipmunk teeth. He decided to have his front teeth pulled, to let his hair grow to cover his ears, and, when he could, to get his name changed. It was in Marquette, he says, that he began making plans to get a college degree and, if he should ever get out, to do something that would be of service to people one way or another. This was probably the kind of reflection he had in mind when he mentioned age twenty-five as the first time he was genuinely aware of himself and of mean-ingful choices.

Karamazov mentions in passing a second effect of the time he spent in the hole—a benefit not quite as benign as the self-knowledge he reported first. He became aware that the law was powerless to punish him any more severely than it already had done:

> In my particular case, there's nothing that they can do to me, short of killing me. If I wanted to walk out of here and kill the Warden tomorrow, there's nothing they can do about it in Michigan. They don't have capital punishment. All they can say is, OK, we got to lock him up [in the hole] for x num-ber of years, which wouldn't be particularly impor-tant to me, and they know that. I've been locked up for as long as two years at one time—in one cell, coming out five minutes a week. And I love it.

Allowing for some exaggeration in that statement, still the Michigan penal system had done its worst and he did not appear to be much shaken by it. I don't know how important

118

this knowledge may have been to Karamazov—or may still be—but it has a rock-bottom quality to it that may underlie his cool courage and brashness. He may have reason to fear other prisoners sometimes, but as for the prison officials, what can they do?

Time in the hole had a third use for Karamazov, related to the first two but not identical with them. It allowed him to test himself, to see how long he could endure. In response to a commonplace remark of mine about prison's being depressing, he said:

I don't know. There's a lot of good things in them too. A lot of things I wouldn't change. I wouldn't really change going to the hole—in the Annex part of it. [At Marquette, the Annex to F Block provides the most desolate segregation.] I wouldn't change that. I found my breaking point there. That's the only place I've ever found where . . . where . . . a situation could overwhelm me. I was in there for about twelve or fourteen days the first time. Then I came out, and I spent one or two days outside, and I went back in again. Now there was no one but me in there, I was the only one in this whole area at the time, so I'm totally secluded, you know. For the first couple of days, what I'd do is I'd take the socks and unravel them. Then I'd make a ball out of another part of them and tie it all together and then see how far I could throw it out. Well, there was shower stalls a good long distance out—probably I'd say a good fifteen, twenty yards, maybe. OK. The shower stalls, they were old ones they didn't use anymore, but they still had the heads on them. And the light above on the bottom of this guard tower, shining down, would project that shadow of the shower head onto the floor right in the middle of the stall, so it made a bull's eye. Well, I'd always try to throw it out there and hit that bull's eye. You know, so many days of that and you say, OK, that's enough of *that*.

I'd make chess boards out of toilet paper and play chess games with myself and all that, but eventually, on the third trip back—cumulative time was into the twenties, twenty-one or twenty-seven days, I don't know which it was—and I started bugging out. I could feel myself going. You know, I'm losing grip on it. And I said, OK, I've got to get out of here. I said, Hey, this is *it*. No more. So I set on the mattress and I made a rat come out of the toilet. I made him so real that I freaked out. And when the cops come back there—now part of it was play acting and part of it was for real, I really was freaking out—I made that rat so real that they could almost see it. They let me out of the hole. But that right there, that was my breaking point. I took a lot of pride in it because I didn't know anybody else that had ever done anything near that long. That was a really weird experience. I can still see that damn rat up on the edge of the toilet thing there.

So far in this chapter, control has meant self-control, the ability to concentrate on the moment when a spider will walk back across a towel or on a ravelled sock tossed and tossed into a shadowy target. It has meant the ability to manage one's own thoughts and feelings so that isolation becomes ineffective as a punishment. Or it has meant control of the spider-and-fly machine, the miniature prison. But his stay in Marquette taught Karamazov control of the real prison as well—the assumptions and constraints of the prison staff, why things are done or not done, how a prisoner can nudge the workings of the prison a little. He learned that endurance can be used actively as well as passively. He and other inmates used it, for example, to force some changes in the hole itself.

I asked Karamazov what the hole was like. He explained that every prison is different, and within a given prison there are degrees of austerity in the cell blocks designated for segregation—all of them known as the hole. In Marquette, when he was there, B Block was ordinary segregation, where men are sent for violation of regulations within the prison. Mainly, their freedom of movement is reduced: they cannot move about the prison as the general population can, going to Recreation or Hobby-Craft, working on the newspaper, talking with other prisoners outdoors in the prison yard, going to work or movies or the prison store. Q Block is sterner segregation, with no recreation periods. The men here are doing long-term segregation; this was where Searl constructed the spider machine. The next step down is F Block where no outside inmates are allowed. The prisoners' only outside human contact is with the prison staff.

But then within F Block there's another part, they call it the Annex. That's back in the back where you get absolutely nothing. Now when I first went back there, there was a cold water faucet coming out into a cement basin, steel boiler-plate to sleep on, you get one blanket, a pair of sox, and a pair of white coveralls. The light is controlled from outside. You got double doors. When they close both doors, you can't talk to anyone, you can't hear anyone. And you don't get any hot water. You don't get any soap. You don't get any toothbrush, any toothpaste. I tell you, you do about seven, maybe ten days in there and eventually your hands—have you ever gone on a camping trip? Where you didn't wash your hands for a couple of days? Imagine what it is now you take, oh, eight, ten days. Your hands get so greasy and sticky—and cold water just won't get it off—that you quit eating. You don't get any kind of utensil to eat with, you eat with your fingers. It's so repulsive that you don't eat anymore. You quit eating.

The final punishment, for those not chastened by isolation and grease, is the blower:

They got a blower system in the back, a great huge squirrel-cage blower. The only purpose it serves—they mounted it loose, loosely mounted on steel and cement blocks—when they turn this thing on it literally vibrates this whole building. You get that constant vibration, and there's air ducts that go back to where it's at, and the noise is so loud, combined with that vibration, that you literally can't think a coherent thought. And they'll run that son of a bitch for twelve, fourteen hours. If he comes back there and you're hollering at someone, or knocking on the wall—you know you work out little knock codes; we used to play chess by code, you know, just to do *something*, because after a while you can't sleep anymore, and become disoriented. The only light you have is what they control, so they control the length of your day and, you know, everything is virtually controlled. But if he hears you making any noise, he'll flip that switch on the blower. And then everybody—you can make more enemies back there. Let them catch you making noise, and everyone in that block will hate you for the rest of the time you're in that prison. They will literally hate you with a passion, it's that bad. You know, you gotta blame it on somebody, and it ends up being that sucker that made the noise.

Eventually, Searl and some other prisoners in Marquette used what they knew about the prison system and about their own powers of endurance to force some changes in the Annex. There were twelve cells in the Annex so twelve long-term prisoners planned to get themselves sent to the Annex and then fast until the prison officials loosened up and rewrote the regulations. I asked him how prisoners could plan a thing like this without the prison officials knowing about it.

> They knew what we were doing. They would sit there and listen to us discuss this thing. And we didn't give a damn. We knew we were going to do it anyway, regardless. So first they told us, "You're not going to the hole." "Are you crazier than hell? We're *going* to the hole." So we started taking the earphones out—they had earphones in that part—we'd take the earphones and throw them at the cops. That didn't do it so we started burning everything on the block, blankets, pillows, everything else. The old horse-hair blankets, they'd been laying around here for two, three years, you know, they're all sweaty—talk about stink. So the damn cops, we're burning the block up and all they do is close all the windows up and go outside, stand outside and look through the window at us. We're in there suffocating in this damn stuff. Worse than tear gas. But we wouldn't let them back in the block, then, see? So we're taking bars of soap and putting them on strings and knocking windows out with them. Pull them back and try to knock another one out. So after two days of that, they finally came back and said, "OK, what do you guys want?" And we said, "We want to go to the hole, it's simple as that." "Why didn't you say so?" you know, and this kind of thing. So we go back to the hole and start our fast.

At least in his telling of it, Searl clearly takes pleasure in this prison combat, this testing of each side by the other. He even seems to admire the shrewdness of the police in closing the windows and letting the prisoners choke on the smoke of their own sweaty blankets. And he enjoyed thinking how to counter that move. When the fast succeeded in improving conditions in the hole, his satisfaction was unmistakable. Presumably, it would have been easy enough to stay out of the hole, but it was a greater challenge to go there deliberately, suffer, and force the officials to change it a little.

We fasted for sixteen days in there, drinking nothing but water. Sixteen whole days. Eventually, on the fifteenth day, the warden came down with two steak sandwiches for each one of us and begged us to please eat those steak sandwiches. We threw them at him. You know what they did next? They came down the sixteenth day, said "Where's your list of demands?" We got hot water and wash cloths and towels and toothpaste and tooth brushes and full meals—they were giving half meals, no drinks or anything—we got everything. We revolutionized it. Then the next week I went back to test it, intentionally went back to the hole, and the sons of bitches had it right back the same way. I hollered out through the vents, "Come on you guys, we got to do it again." It stopped right there. They come back there with the hot water and soap and everything else. Turned it right around.

12.

Julie: Her Children

After six years of marriage, Julie Searl divorced Tommy in 1971, while he was in Jackson Prison, but she did not shift to his brother, the winning horse, right away. After she left Tommy, she saw a good deal of Bob Melos, whom she had also known in high school. He had been Ralph's best friend. When Tommy was arrested and charged with the rape and murder of four young women, the name Searl took on a foul taste in everyone's mouth. Tommy's sons, especially his oldest son David, were treated with contempt by the other children, and Julie herself hated to say her name. Immediately after the trial, she married Bob. "I thought I would change the name to Melos and see if that worked any better. Besides, there was part of me that needed to be discussing Ralph." Julie bore Bob Melos a daughter, Rosey, but after two years, their marriage disintegrated, too. In March 1975, she married Ralph Searl, who by that time was Luke Karamazov.

In August 1977, nine months after our first conversation, I talked with Julie Karamazov a second time. A lot had happened in the interval. Julie and her family were no longer living in the tiny house by the tracks on Mill Street. They had moved to a pleasant two-story house on Rice Street, across

from a public park a couple of blocks from the center of
Ionia. When I had first spoken with her, Julie and her children were living on checks from Aid to Dependent Children
and on a little money Julie made as a clerk in the Ionia High
School under the CETA program. Now, in August, she had a
full-fledged job with the County Department of Social Services. She seemed more relaxed and confident. Her children
ran in from the park from time to time to see if supper was
ready and ran out again, cheerfully enough, when she told
them she was still busy.

She spoke about the things most on her mind: her son
David, who had been deeply hurt by the neighbors' insults
at the time of his father's trial, her marriage to Luke Karamazov, and her new job. David had been seeing psychologists at the Child Guidance Clinic since shortly after the
trial. Julie didn't know it at the time, but they saw in him
severe signs of childhood schizophrenia and were inclined to
place the boy in an institution. "But they knew," she said, "I
was so upset they couldn't approach this subject to me without my taking my kids and running—which I would have
done—so they decided to work with me instead." They did
that, with her cooperation, and the results were satisfying.
They could hardly believe the progress that had been made,
she told me. David was not completely well yet, but the
progress had been remarkable.

I asked whether this progress was the result of her treat-
ing David differently than she had before.

> I think it is a result of being settled myself. I am not
> searching for anything anymore. Dr. Morris told
> me—I went to him and said, "Can I marry Luke?
> What's it going to do to my boys?" And he said, "I
> wish you would meet somebody from Arizona,
> some tall dark cowboy with a cowboy hat." But I
> don't like cowboy hats. He went up and I don't
> know how many sessions he had with Luke. He
> came back and he said, "The only way your kids

are going to be happy is if you're happy. You're one of those girls that's not going to be happy unless you're with Luke. You fell for the guy, unfortunately you fell too hard." He said, "Marry him." When I went in to show them I'd had my blood test, both doctors gave me a great big hug.

Luke works with the boys, he writes to the boys, he talks to them. He does more for them up there than anyone's ever done for them anyplace else, including Tommy. I don't know where Tommy's working out of. He doesn't correspond with the boys. He doesn't seem to have any desire to have pictures of them. He's just shown no interest in the kids. With David especially, the question will come up, where's my real dad? Why doesn't he write to us?

No one in our house says anything against their father, no one. I want them to be raised with the idea that he was sick, that it wasn't the father side of him that committed these crimes. I don't want them to hate him. I want them to love—that is their father—but I don't want them to love the act. I want them to hate the act. David especially— he just realized, before we moved, what rape is. I've always censored the kids' TV shows, and this night in particular I was busy with some friends that had come over and didn't pay any attention to what was on TV. By the time I realized what had happened on TV, it was too late to change the station. The people that were there were calling the guy on TV a "sick-o" and "ought-to-be-shot" and this type of thing, not knowing anything about our history, what we've been through. After they left that night, David wanted to know if Tommy had also committed rape. And we sat down, David and I, and discussed what rape was. He's just now coming to the age where I know he's going to have more and more questions. I just hope I'm strong enough to give him the right answers.

Julie sees many similarities between David and Tommy. Neither one is good at seeing himself objectively. "He can't look at himself. Tommy never could do that either. Neither of them could ever look in a mirror. Hopefully, David is going to come out of that." They seem to have a similar interest in science, especially astronomy. "Science and the stars. He had no way of knowing that Tommy was this way. That's just where his interests are himself. He hasn't gotten to girls yet. . . . But on the other hand, David can be the most understanding of all my boys. David has felt the most from this whole thing. It's grown David a lot beyond his years."

That summer Julie had talked with the counselor at the junior high school David would be attending in the fall. Seventh grade, she said, is supposed to be the hardest year, anyway, and she wanted to pave as much of the road as she could for David. The year before, no one at the school had taken time to read his records. When she went in for a conference, "they called him a brat, fighter, unrealistic, and everything else, but they knew nothing about where he'd come from, what he'd been through. They didn't see the progress that had been made. They were throwing all this negative shit on this kid, constantly."

> This is a verbal kid. Tommy was always verbal. He looks like Tommy, I'm sure you saw that. The day's going to come when he's going to want to go to Marquette. I know I can't send him now, with Tommy telling everyone he's innocent. I cannot allow the boys to grow up hating the police, the authorities, this type of thing. This is what would be the result if they were allowed to go to Marquette. I'm glad he doesn't correspond with the kids—that way I don't have to keep anything from them. I cannot at this time in their lives allow

them to have anything to do with him. Maybe he knows this. Maybe that's why he doesn't write, I don't know. But it's worked out for the best. And when the day comes, I'll just hope.

She hopes, too, that there will never be an appeal that will open the case up again for retrial. James Gregart, the Kalamazoo County Prosecutor, assured her that there would never be any appeals. "I hope he's telling me that based on what he knows, not on trying to get me to relax." Possibly, she thinks, Ionia is far enough from Kalamazoo so that a new trial would not overwhelm them there as it did when they lived within a mile or two of the courthouse.

Being there in Kalamazoo with it, it was hell. Maybe it would be different being up here away from it, maybe the news wouldn't be that great, that sensational. But I know David couldn't handle it again. I question myself whether *I'm* up to it. It seems harder for me to go back and think about yesterday than it was for me at the time to live through it. But we've come up here, we've started new, we've got good things going for us. I've got a good job. The kids are being able to take pride in themselves. No one's making fun of them. They seem to—I don't know, they just seem to be— happy.

Julie was hired in Social Services as an aide "to sit at a desk and do paper work," but now she is a child welfare worker, helping to place kids in foster homes, to work with foster parents and with kids while they're in foster care. She sometimes works with the Protective Services staff, looking into reports that children are being neglected or abused. "I've just started getting into the delinquency aspect of it, working with delinquent kids. A little bit of everything. And it's important to me. I think that if somebody had been there twenty years ago, we wouldn't be sitting here today. My

129

job's very, very important for that reason. Luke keeps telling me, 'I gave signs, I gave warning signals—if somebody had been there.' And I keep thinking, this is my job now. If I can help one kid, you know, I've done something."

My kids love it. They love knowing that mom's working and not drawing ADC. They take pride. We've been able to get furniture, you know? We've been able to get extra things that they need in school. And they keep telling me, we're rich now. We're by no means rich, but if they want a dollar to go to the show, we can do it now. They're getting off on the fact that they're not going to take school lunches this year. For all these years, it's been free lunches. This year they're going to carry their sack lunch. It's beautiful to see these kids proud for a change.

When I first took the job with Social Services, I thought who gave me the authority to do this, who gave me the authority to supervise visits, to decide whether mom was real or dad was real. It really bothered me. I talked with Pauline about it, she's my boss, and the thing that kept coming up again and again is that I've lived through so many of these experiences that maybe I am in a better position to help some of these people. I've been there on ADC, I've been there when you didn't have the money to let your kid go to the show, I've been there when all kinds of hell was coming down around me, and I can feel what these people are feeling now, you know? It's a scary job.

I asked Julie how it was, being married to a man in prison. It is hard, she said, not knowing what the future is going to bring. Shortly before I spoke with her, Karamazov had petitioned the State of Indiana to waive the detainer it had placed on him, and Indiana had done that. Now, if he should be released in Michigan, he would not have to stand

130

trial in Indiana. Julie got excited about this news, thinking she could "see daylight." But Luke didn't encourage her to hope much. "He won't allow me even that excitement, you know?" The Prosecutor, James Gregart, tells her that he will never get out.

Yet I don't believe that. I guess I don't want to. I've said five years for the past six years. And it never moves. Next year at this time it's going to be five years, I know that. But I can handle that in my head. We can sit together for twelve hours—we did yesterday. And it's not a thing of watching the clock or the time dragging; the time goes fast. We have these things to talk about, we have enough to keep us talking. Everybody asks me that question. I don't know how to answer. I'm happy, I can say that. I don't live in fear that tomorrow's going to bring something bad.

My biggest hangup is that god-damn cop. He told me after one of the days in court: "Better have your boys' brains checked. It runs in the genes. They probably inherited something." That idea stuck with me for a long, long time. I guess I've let go of that. I've finally been able to say, "That guy deserved the slap across the face I gave him." But we went through this. More than one person told me on different occasions to have my boys' brains checked. But I don't look for it in my boys. If I look for it, it's going to be there. If I look hard enough, I'm eventually going to find it. So I just accept them, that they are *my kids*. That's it. They're going to grow up normal, healthy kids. They're good kids.

13.

Tommy and Julie

Although Ralph and Tommy Searl grew up in the same family with only a year's difference in their ages, although they both married the same woman and both were convicted of the murder of several people, their personalities are very different. We have already seen Karamazov's self-sufficiency, competence, and cool authority, his persuasiveness, his fearlessness, and his apparently low levels of inner conflict, regret, or guilt—a cluster of traits that would lead psychologists to identify him as a psychopath, or, to use the term currently preferred, an antisocial personality. Since his transfer to Ionia (and his name change), he has become more controlled and dependable, more consistently part of the social organization of the prison. Still, his actions fit many of the patterns described by Hervey Cleckley in *The Mask of Sanity*, William and Joan McCord in *The Psychopath*, and Theodore Millon in *Disorders of Personality* (see Appendix).

Tommy is another matter. I drove up to Marquette to talk with him in August 1977. Since it was a long drive, I stayed for three days, recording Tommy's conversation for several hours each day. While I was there, I also talked briefly with the prison counselor who knew Tommy best and with the Deputy Warden who also remembered Ralph—and showed me the chessboard-crossbow that we will get to in the next chapter. Tommy is built about the way his brother is, perhaps five feet nine inches, slender and muscular, but instead of the long hair, beard, and dark glasses which give Luke a mysterious, slightly sinister look, Tommy wears a crew cut and clear, squarish steel-rimmed glasses. When I met him he was neat and clean shaven, wearing a blue leisure suit over a light blue turtleneck.

I did not find Tommy frightening—though I realize my reactions might have been different if I had been a woman. The prison officials reported that he was a thoroughly cooperative prisoner, not intimidating or dangerous as his brother had been. In fact, the prison counselor didn't know exactly what to make of Tommy's good deeds. "His ideas—they're good but they're *different*." For example, the telephone company has an arrangement whereby inmates can make collect calls to their families and others. One year at Christmas, Tommy wrote to the telephone company asking how many operators handled these calls from prison—forty-five as it turned out—so that he could give each of them a gift as thanks for their courteous handling of the prisoners' calls. The gifts were ink drawings, tracings more or less, which he made by projecting a picture from a book or magazine onto the wall of his cell and copying it in his own hand. I saw several of his drawings in the prison handcraft shop: a squirrel, a mare and colt (the mare in brown ink, the colt in black), two boys on an ox, knights jousting in front of a castle, three roses in red, green, and black ink. They were skillful and attractive, worthy gifts, but the whole project seemed odd. It didn't particularly win him the admiration of the other prisoners, and the prison staff were suspicious at first, wondering what he was up to. Tommy himself complained about this suspicion: "The best way to get out of prison is to make some trouble. If you're nice all the time, they think you're conning them."

I, too, wondered about these good deeds. Tommy told me that he was a minister in the Universal Life Church.

(Anyone could be a minister, he said; all you had to do was write and ask to be ordained.) He showed me letters from Sister Marguerite and her fourth grade students at St. Agnes School in Ashford, Ohio. As a result of Tommy's correspondence, the class took on the Marquette prisoners as a sort of school project, making about fifty feet of murals to decorate the prison visiting room at Christmas time, preparing a Christmas radio program (which was aired on WDMJ-FM in Marquette), and writing letters to individual prisoners, especially Tommy. In return, Tommy sent one of his drawings to each of the children and kept up a correspondence with the children as well as Sister Marguerite. Some members of the community got in on the project as well. After my visit to Marquette, Nancy Beckwith, an Ashford woman who was training to be a nurse, wrote to me about Tommy, saying that she had been writing to him for three years and referring to him as her "closest friend." (Both she and Sister Marguerite had visited Tommy in prison.) Clearly Tommy got satisfaction from this connection with Ashford. He showed me snapshots of the mural the children sent and articles about the school-prison project that were published in various Ohio newspapers, including the Port Clinton *News Herald* and the Toledo *Blade*, and a couple of Catholic journals, *Our Sunday Visitor* and the *Catholic Chronicle*. I remembered that he had no contact with his family. Julie was now married to Ralph. Tommy never heard from his sons or wrote to them. He had taken up with another woman, Dora Bonor, during the summer of the murders and married her after he had been in prison for six months; but now they were separated, estranged. Ashford, and for a moment myself, constituted his link with the outside world.

During my visit, Tommy talked at length about his childhood, riding bikes and sleds down East Main hill, shooting sling shots and BB guns, fighting with Ralph, climbing the train trestle over the Kalamazoo River and racing to get across ahead of the train, being beaten with a 2 by 4 by his drunken father, being told by a teacher in first or second grade to sit down and shut up—and doing it for the rest of his time in school. He talked about his alleged rapes and murders, talked fast, I thought, as though he wanted to get the whole story on tape exactly the way it was—or the way he wished it had been.

He talked about Julie, and the talk had quite a different tone than when he was talking about the telephone operators and Ashford. He and she had been in school together, and he wrote to her, along with ten other girls, he said, when he was in the navy. Then he became more and more attached to Julie, but their relationship was violent from the beginning. "Julie was always an extremely impulsive female. She would slap you in a second if she didn't get what she wanted. I was taught to be too much of a gentleman to hit women. I never struck a woman. I never slapped a girl, even my sister."

"Julie would slap you and say she's sorry but not really be sorry. She would be impulsive. She would swing in a second." He told of an incident shortly before they were married. Julie was driving her Oldsmobile, with Tommy's younger sister Sally in the car with her. Tommy's mother wanted Sally to come home, so Tommy took off after the girls in his Mustang. Julie knew he was following her and they had a high-speed chase, Tommy going over a bridge so fast the Mustang left the ground. By and by, the girls stopped, Tommy grabbed Sally, and Julie took off, mad, slamming through a stop sign. Back at their house, according to Tommy's account, Julie was still angry:

> She jumped out of the car and she started cussing and started yelling, and she said something to my mother. And I stood up and said, don't say nothing to my mother, just drop it. I said, Sally's home now, that's it. Just go home. And she hauled off and hit me. I'm telling you she slapped me, wham, threw my neck aside, pulled the muscle in the side of my neck. Well, I said, if you're big enough to do that why don't you go ahead and hit the other

side? And I was mad, but I wasn't, you know—I
was just mad. And she did—hit me on the other
side and pulled the muscles on the other side. I
couldn't move my neck. For a good two weeks,
two, three weeks, I could not move my neck. She
pulled all the muscles. That's how hard she hit me,
she put all she had into it. She weighed as much as
I did then. I weighed 135 and that's what she
weighed. . . . I was so mad I was seeing black, but
I didn't hit her back. You don't hit women.

For reasons I couldn't fully explain, the narrative made
me uncomfortable. The account seemed too emphatic, over
dramatized. Tommy didn't seem at ease telling it. But I nod-
ded and kept the tape recorder going, and he continued with
the sorry history of his relationship with Julie. He confronted
her with his supposed discovery that she was not a virgin,
and later, after they were married, he returned from work
unexpectedly and found a man, their former high school
class president, in the house with Julie. She claimed the visit
was innocent, but Tommy checked with a neighbor who
said, "He comes when you leave." "That destroyed my marriage," Tommy said, "destroyed any truth that I had in Julie,
but I still loved her. I would have killed for her. I told her if
the guy ever came around again, when I wasn't here, I'd
hurt him."

But he also talked of his own infidelities—which led to
discussion of his sex drive and rape and the changes that his
arrests and imprisonment may have caused in him. He had
an affair, he said, with Julie's sister's girl friend and with a
girl he met when he was working as a truck driver.

I had sex with her, let's put it that way. I didn't
have an affair, I just had sex with her. I had a
strong sex drive. But I don't believe in hurting
women. I don't believe that what's given away free
should be taken by force. This is one thing that
angers me so bad at the charges that I'm charged

with. But the police look at it, every woman they talk to that knows me tells them, Hey, he's got a, you know, strong sex drive. The police look at it as if he's got a strong sex drive, he must be a rapist. He must be a fanatic about sex. They feel if you have sex once a day or twice a day that you're a sex fiend. This is the impression I get of the people that stand in judgment of me. I don't believe that what you can have for free you have the right to take. And I believe that people that you don't know, you have no business approaching them. But that's my philosophy, that's me inside.

Or at least it was before this bit. If I got out of here today, I don't know what I would do. Because I haven't been around women. I don't know whether I've changed. Because I haven't experienced any change. But I will say this, that the women guards that are in here, and there's two, I can look at them and I feel no urge to attack them. So I don't think I've changed, but I don't know. I know I've changed to the point where now if I got out I would hurt some cops. I would hurt some cops. To me, any cop is fair game, from what they did to me. That's something I know. I know that for a fact. Take it for what you want. I'm being honest. Completely honest. I don't believe I can tell you fairy tales and have you write anything that's going to amount to anything. If I tell you nice little stories and stuff like this, that'd be fine, but I don't believe you're interested in fairy tales. You're interested in facts.

At the time Tommy was telling me this, I felt the urgency of his manner, but I didn't pay attention to the remarkable transitions that led him, in a minute or two, from an affair with Julie's sister's friend to hurting cops, nor did I notice his protestations of honesty, his willingness to confess to crimes that have not yet been committed, his speaking of them as fact—his hurting some cops in the hypothetical future. After this, the facts led him back to Julie and the most violent episodes in their marriage, the fights that Julie had spoken of earlier:

You're interested in facts. I'm trying to give them to you just as clear as I can remember. And Julie continued striking me, continued hitting me, constantly, that's one problem we had, that's why I kept leaving, because she would strike me and that would be it, I would want to hurt her. That'd be it. And I'd pull up instead. One incident, she slammed the bedroom door and tore the hinges on it. We had had a row about something and she tore the hinges on the door. I told her don't do it again. She slapped me in the face and spit in my face. After that was over, I never—yeah, I did strike her. She slapped me in the face and spit in my face. She was standing up by the side of the bed. I was in the bedroom. And I said don't you *ever* slam that bedroom door again. She's standing up next to the bed. And that's when she slapped me and spit in my face. And I lost control. At that second, I struck. I put my hands, thumbs touching, together. And hit her in the collar bones, just like this. And I hit her so hard, with such an upward force, that I picked her clean off her feet, and laid her on the bed. The only thing that was hanging over the bed was her chin. She was laying completely flat on her back. I jumped on top of her, straddling her, and I just started slapping her face, just kept slapping back and forth, back and forth, until my rage had been worked off. And that's the first time I ever touched Julie. First time. I left.

As he remembers it, Tommy then took an apartment across town for a while. Two women he had grown up with,

139

two lesbians, moved in with him. He had an affair, he said, with one of the women, and they moved out. About the same time, Tommy remembers going to the police for help. Julie had left their son David with her father while she was at work, with instructions not to let Tommy come near him. So Tommy went to the police to get his son back, and the memory lets him say again how bitter and mistrustful he has become. "The police had to chase him downtown and bring him back to the station, you know, to take my son from him. If I was in the frame of mind then as I am now, I would have just ran him off the road and taken my son. I would have hurt the guy. But I was peace-loving back then. Still trying to pick and live the good life as everybody expects you to, nonviolent and all that stuff, get the police to handle your fights for you. Now I know there's no solution to that, you bust a guy's head so he respects you and not the police. That's the only way you can get anything."

Before long, Tommy moved back with Julie and they had the big fight, the one that sent him travelling north across the Upper Peninsula, through Minnesota, and finally to prison in Cheyenne. Again, Tommy doesn't remember exactly what set off the fight but the bedroom door comes in this time, too, as a sort of symbolic cause of his rage. He had intercepted the letters from his brother Ralph, in prison, to David and Julie, the love letters, and he had found Julie's letter in reply.

This was the second time that I lost my temper with Julie. It was after I put the bedroom door in solid oak. I put the jamb in solid oak so she couldn't tear it off. It took me two days to do it but I did it. Something else happened, I don't know what it was, we had a fight over something. She did the same thing: she went in the room and she slammed the door. And I told her not to do it again, I said don't you *ever* slam that door again. She was in the bed. I didn't lose my temper then. I went in the bed. She got up and went in the other bedroom, the spare bedroom, and went to sleep on the spare bed. That was Sally's room, Sally lived with us for a while. I went in the room. And I said you're not sleeping here, you're sleeping back in there, in that bedroom. That's the agreement we made when we were married. And she rolled over and she spit at me. She said, I wouldn't sleep with you, you son of a bitch. And when she said that again, I lost my temper and my fist started up high, just as high as I could reach—all the way down, half of me was pushing just as hard as I could, the other half of me was pulling just as hard as I could to stop. Then I hit her in the mouth, almost knocked this tooth out of her mouth, knocked it loose. I think that's the last time I hit Julie. That's the last time.

In discussing this rage and violence, Tommy comes back again to the behavior of a gentleman, that bit of propriety that seems so inadequate in the turbulence of his relationship with Julie. The bedroom door may have represented a similar fragment of truth, something he could hold onto, a conjugal right. When he cannot sort out the surge and racket of the actual argument, he can remember and understand the bedroom door. In fact, the thank-you notes to the telephone operators and the correspondence with fourth graders in Ashford may have a similar standing: pieces of certainty when much of his life seems to be a confusion of impulse and choice, fact and invention. Here is the gentleman once more:

There's a point when you're taught to be a gentleman that you don't hit women, there's a point that you learn that it's not gentlemen and ladies no more, it's self defense, it's such a thing as self defense. If I had struck Julie before we got married, the first time she ever hit me, if I had hauled off and knocked her down, I don't think I'd ever been hit again. I don't think she'd ever hit me again. But hindsight is always better than foresight. You can always see what you should have done, never what you should do. What you should do is never that clear. You have six hundred options, and you pick one of them, whichever you're tending towards.

Tommy began making a list of the reasons why things went wrong: "Julie did not respect me, number one. Number two, Julie, I believe—I accused her one time of marrying me because my name was Searl, not because I was Tommy Searl, and not because I was Tommy." I asked if he thought she liked Ralph right from the beginning. "I think she did." But then he was not sure. He thought she loved both of them. At first she respected him more than Ralph because he was older. And at the start she had more feelings, more sexual feelings for him. But mentally she was in love with Ralph. Finally, he came back to reasons one and two:

> As the years progressed, and as our marriage went downhill, and as she saw more of me and I knew more of her, she lost her respect for me, which happens in most marriages anyway. But when there's the contributing factor of her being in love with another guy, it just tore it apart, it disintegrated. I'm not going to apologize for anything I did, and I'm not going to condemn her for anything she did. Maybe if I'd handled things differently, it'd been different. But that's history, it's history. I still love her. If she walked in this room today, after all she did to me, lying on the stand, getting me accused of this, inciting the incidents we had in our life with the slappings, the love letters to Ralph—I'm not mentioning any of the things I did—after her doing her share to destroy the marriage, if she walked in this room today, I

would have a hell of a fight to keep from putting my arms around her and kissing her. I'm serious. She means that much to me.

On an impulse, I asked Tommy if he ever had dreams, real dreams at night. He remembered one and told me about it, a dream that had to do with Julie. The dream itself seemed to me poignant and direct, one of the most spontaneous things he had offered in our conversations; and his interpretation of it seemed to me sensible and sane, properly tentative. Yet the discussion of the dream prompted him to worry about his mental health, about the "dearth" and loneliness of prison, and the hazards of an active imagination there.

Yeah, I have dreams like everybody else. Cold nights I don't dream that much. I dream but I don't remember them on cold nights because I sleep better. But now if I take naps I have lots of dreams. I dreamt I'd been with Julie, lots of times. Julie—as a matter of fact, if I have a dream which involves a woman, it usually relates around Julie. I have dreams about prison here. I think I have normal dreams, I haven't ever seen anything unusual. See, I read *Psychology Today* and I try to keep myself mentally healthy. So I try to remember what my dreams are and I try to evaluate them. You know, why would you think that way or what is the reason behind that, like if I start a dream that—. I had one dream that stands out pretty strong: I started to dream that I was at a party. I met Julie. We left the party and went to her apartment I think it was, or her house, and we—either we had a drink or something like that, we were doing something— and the next thing I know we're in the bedroom and we started to have sex, in other words she was taking her clothes off, and she got in bed and I remember looking down at her and she had the body of a child, a little girl, and I remember stopping and raring back and asking, what's wrong, and I looked at her face and it wasn't Julie no more and I don't know who the girl was.

But now back when I was a kid, back when I was eight, nine, ten maybe, my buddy Douglas, one of his little sisters—he was up in the bedroom, now Ralph and I went up to get him up and the little girl was running around in her panties. Now the youngest girl—we were always talking about Let me do it, let me do it. We didn't know what "do it" meant. We didn't know about sex. Hell, I didn't know anything about sex till I got in the service, or actually just before I got in the service. I didn't know anything about intercourse. Sex to us was looking at a girl, that's all, that was sex, nothing else. But she got in bed with me. I think I had my clothes on then, she didn't have nothing on, see, and I remember looking down at her—and I think I might have supplanted her for Julie. But why? I've never been able to figure it out, why would I supplant that little girl for Julie? That kept me cooking for a week or two on that, that's why it still lodges in my mind. I wondered about that. Maybe that was a psychological urge to have Julie and go back to before our problems, back when we were younger. Maybe that was something to do with it, I don't know. Why wouldn't I put Julie back in there when I first met her? Why did I make her go back to a young girl who had no pubic hair and nothing like that, no breasts?

But I try to keep myself mentally active. I don't believe in letting myself vegetate. It's so easy to do in here because nothing happens. Nothing happens. Nobody cares about you. Nobody cares whether you come out that day or stay in your house or whether you go out and run around the yard or—you got a few acquaintances, you got casual acquaintances but nobody to be close to, nobody that really cares. Maybe, you know, there's a few homosexual relationships in here, where if you stab that guy, this guy's going to stab you back, something like that. Generally, inmate-wise, there's just no closeness, there's just nothing there. This is why I try to keep myself active, because I don't want to bug out. I don't want to go around a corner. And it's easy to do here. Especially if you're active-minded. If you've got an active imagination and stuff like that, it's easy to go out to lunch, it's easy. Guys that don't have no imagination, just plod along every day, they could do six hundred years and have no problem. It's the guys that are active mentally that go around the corner. Pretty soon, it's just a dearth, there's nothing there. And if you can't create it, you've got to create it the other way. Out to lunch you go. I don't *think* I'm out to lunch yet—might have went for a sandwich now and then.

14.

The Loan Shark and the Crossbow

Toward the end of his stay in Marquette, Ralph Searl became the craftsman again, this time manufacturing one of the most elaborate and deadly of the hundreds of weapons that have been produced illegally inside the prison. He speaks of it as a crossbow. As he tells the story, the crossbow was made to be used on a fellow prisoner, a barber whom Searl and some other inmates had set up as their loan shark.

A loan shark in here, the first thing he has to have, of course, is money. This guy had some money. Now the second thing that he needs is somebody trustworthy to loan the money to and get it back, in a specified time. Now in that particular prison they get 25 percent so if I borrow a dollar, I bring you back a dollar and a quarter, OK? And it's compound interest. If I miss a payment, then it's interest on a dollar and a quarter rather than just interest on a dollar. It's a spiralling thing. So what we would do, we'd go to him and borrow a hundred dollars, and bring him back a hundred and twenty-five, say two weeks later. That's the usual run. Then he has a hundred and twenty-five to loan out. Hundred and twenty-five would give him, what, thirty-one and a quarter, loaning that hundred and a quarter again. So in time he becomes the richest one there. For five years we maintain this guy, we're his steady reliable customers. When he gives us the money, he knows it's good as gold, you know. Like loaning it to the bank, you're going to get it back.

Whenever you're running a poker game you have to have a steady, reliable source of money. Because what happens is, if I run a poker game, you come and play. All right, every pot I get ten percent of that pot. For that, I maintain a table and a cloth to play on and buy the cards and buy the food, whatever is needed, OK? It can add up to a pretty good stake. The only problem is, though, if you come to the game with twenty dollars, let's say, and you lose the twenty, then I'm morally obligated to *loan* you money to keep playing. It's only good business for me.

So the barber provided the loan money to whoever was running the game. But the poker players spent some time in the hole, and when they came out, ready to get the game going again, they found that the loan shark had changed the terms:

This guy he runs a little thing on us. Yeah, you can get the money but you've got to put all your valuables in hock, for security. We're not going for this. So it ends up, we're standing around, every yard period, looking at this guy, talking among ourselves, you know, we're going to have to get this sucker. Just to pay him back. So what we figured on doing was, one of us would kill him, right when the whistle blew, and the rest that lived in that particular block, would hit his cell which would be open, and we would take back all of our security, plus whatever he happened to have in his strong box. We were just going to take it all. So what we had to have was some efficient way of taking him out, hopefully without being caught. So I come up with the idea of making a crossbow. Being a mechanical genius, you know, I just fell into that channel of activity.

I have seen this crossbow. It is kept in the warden's office in Marquette, part of a fantastic array of improvised weapons confiscated from inmates in the prison. What distinguishes this one is that it is disguised as a chessboard. It is of normal chessboard size but hollow, about an inch thick. On the top, dark and light squares of wood are inlaid to make the playing surface. The bottom is covered with a piece of masonite and black oilcloth. Around the edges, holes have been drilled every few inches and filled with sections of dark dowel, making a decorative pattern. It appears to be—and is—a hollow chessboard.

Inside there is a track, above and below, like the track that guides the arrow in a crossbow. The track leads to a hole in the edge of the board, one of the decorative holes but with the dark dowel missing. The missile, a three-inch stainless steel nail sanded to a fine point and set in a smaller dowel, travels down the track and out through the hole in the edge of the board. It is propelled by an extremely heavy rubber band, the kind they use in hobby craft to hold together pieces of wood while they are being glued. The rubber band is fastened to the edge of the board, at the front on each side, rather like the string on a bow; it is pulled to the back of the board as the machine is cocked. Searl devised, from clock parts, a simple trigger, so that the missile could be released by pushing in a dowel that protruded slightly on the side of the board. There is no question about the effectiveness of the weapon. The Deputy Warden told me that he himself had fired the machine, with the rubber band pulled only halfway back, and the nail went through the three-quarter inch pine of his office door. But Searl delayed when it came to actually using the crossbow on the loan shark.

> I don't know if I was bluffing, because I kept telling the guys, you know, I want it just a hair stronger. Just give me a little more time. I don't know if I actually wanted it stronger but I know it was strong enough to go through his skull. The theory was I was going to be walking behind this guy, and when they blew the whistle, while the whistle was still blowing, cause it blew for about thirty seconds or a minute, continuous, while that whistle was blowing I was going to shoot him in the back of the head, with this crossbow. Then just walk past him, because no one would know what hit him. I figured I could hit him from about seven, eight feet behind him. And before anyone really knew why he had fallen, I'd be past him and in the block, and the board was such that I could dismantle it, the track and everything. I could just pull all the guts out of it and throw them away, and it would be nothing but a hollow chessboard. There wouldn't be any way to really attach it to being what it was. But I really don't think that I was ever going to go through with it.

While Searl was delaying, word came that his appeal to the Supreme Court had been successful and he was to be returned to Kalamazoo for retrial. The local radio station carried this news, and the next night the police came in his cell, shook it down, and confiscated the crossbow. His conjecture is that one of the other inmates who was in on the plot told on him to get some favors for himself. When the informer heard that Searl would be leaving, he was afraid he might miss his chance, so he went to the officials right away. At any rate, the loan-shark barber was not murdered, and the chessboard-crossbow became an exhibit in the warden's office.

15.

Tommy in Prison

Tommy Searl hoped that I would undertake an investigation to prove that he was innocent of the four rape-murders that he had been convicted of. Even before I went to Marquette to meet him, he sent me the name of a nineteen-year-old man who was charged with attempted rape in Kalamazoo and later hung himself in his cell at the Kalamazoo County Jail. This might be the person, Searl later explained, who committed the rapes and murders for which *he* was imprisoned.

Searl has consistently maintained that he did not commit the rapes and murders. The case against him depended heavily on the testimony of Kerry Weiser, who confessed to taking part, with Tommy, in three of the rape-murders and who reported hearing Tommy talk about the fourth one. (As a plea bargain, he was allowed to plead guilty to a single charge of second degree murder in exchange for providing evidence for the prosecution of Tommy. He is now serving time in Jackson prison.) Under examination by Tommy's attorney, Weiser admitted to violating the terms of his Juvenile Court probation, escaping twice from the Kalamazoo County Juvenile Home, being kicked out of school, stealing eighteen to twenty cars, and committing half a dozen burglaries. He was not an ideal witness. Yet his testimony was detailed, and it was corroborated by evidence uncovered by careful police work. The blanket covering the bodies of Nancy Harte and Cornelia Davault was identified as Tommy's. The rope that was used to strangle one of the women was found to match the anchor rope on Searl's stepfather's boat—rope that Tommy had given his stepfather. A sheriff's deputy had actually stopped Tommy at what later turned out to be the time and place of Jennifer Curran's murder. Tommy was coming out of the woods, acting suspiciously. The deputy questioned him, then followed his van and met him several more times as Tommy circled around on the back roads near Comstock. Gradually, the evidence accumulated until the case became convincing, in spite of the dubiousness of the prosecution's chief witness. Juries found Tommy guilty of the rape and murder of Cynthia Kohls and Jennifer Curran, and on the advice of his attorney he pled no contest in the case of the Chicago women. He was sentenced to four life terms.

Tommy told me that he assumes even his mother and sister believe him to be guilty. Yet he maintains his innocence. My own impression is that he is urgently and persistently rethinking the past, going over the events in his mind and rearranging them, changing them so that the story comes out the way it ought to have been rather than the way it was. The episode of the torn note may serve as an example. On January 1, 1973, when Tommy was being held in the Kalamazoo County Jail awaiting trial, two guards came into his cell and found in the toilet bowl the torn-up pieces of a note in Tommy's handwriting. Pieced together, it read:

> Do you know any married women who could use $500.00 for taking the stand and saying she was with me on the night of the Kohls killing, one who would have a reason to remember that (whatever the reason was) night that will stand up in court and also remember I had a Bandaid on my left

cheek and told her I scratched it while tearing down a garage? It has to be a Sat. night I was with her. She must be strong so the cops can't break her down no matter what they say or do. Also she will have to go to the newspaper office (*Gazette*) and look in the past issue for the date and all the back pictures of me so she will know me when she sees me. Let me know as soon as you can as all visits and phone calls in new jail are to be taped. . . . The money will come when my feet hit the streets.

When I asked Tommy about the note, he had an explanation. He had been in the County Jail for almost four months, and, in order to pass the time, he and some other prisoners worked out a numerical code so they could pass messages to each other from cell to cell. When an inmate received a coded note, he would have to transcribe it, letter by letter, to see what was being said. Here is Tommy's account of the incriminating note asking to buy an alibi:

Every note had to be transcribed, completely. I'm sitting in there, note snuck under the back door. So I go ahead and copied it. I'm waiting for a shower. I copied the note down and it says, I'm supposed to buy—to get whatchacallit, to get some gals—I said I didn't write that. I didn't write nothing like this. I ripped it up. I said, it looks like a setup. And I ripped it up and threw it in the toilet—I didn't flush the toilet. That's where the note come from. I told my attorney that at the time. He didn't believe me. I don't expect anybody to believe me. Because you got to be in that jail to really experience this and know what's happening. You got to be in a situation like that. That's the only thing that kept me going was having things like that going, being able to communicate with people. Otherwise they would have broke me. They knew I was doing that and they slipped one in on me and they got me. That's

all. There had been two or three notes before that,
but I had flushed those. That one I didn't. If I'd have
wrote it for real I *know* I'd have take and flushed it.
There'd been nothing laying around.

I asked if he thought some other inmate had sent him
the false note in code.

I don't know who it was. It's a steel door, that was
at the end of my cell. You could reach through a
grill, through wire bars like this, and you could
slide a piece of paper underneath the door and
communicate that way. Somebody slipped it under
there. Who was it? It could have been a cop in the
cell, I don't know. Could have been just the run of
snitches [some prisoner collaborating with the po-
lice]. All I know is what I ended up with. And I'm
the only one in the cell. Seems funny they come
busting in right then, right when I threw it in the
toilet. I laid back real quick. When the key hit the
door? I laid back real quick. Never dawned on me
that I didn't flush the toilet. Furthermore, why, if it
was circumstances, why wasn't it just one cop
come in to take me to the shower like he usually
does. There was three of them out there. Two of
them come in the cell, one took me to the shower. I
don't know. I don't know what the circumstances
were. It's one of those things. You see it from one
side, but you don't know what *really* happened. If
I'd been seeing the whole thing I'd probably tell
you more, but I don't know any more. I don't
know what else happened.

As Tommy said, it *is* hard to believe this—that the torn-
up note was the decoding of a message sent from another
cell. My impression is that it took a good deal of energy for
Tommy himself to believe it—and to fill in the details in his
mind so that it might become convincing.

Much has been written about criminal psychopaths or antisocial personalities, and psychologists readily recognize the characteristic marks in a person like Ralph Searl, even though he now presents an unusually dependable and controlled variation on the type. Tommy is no psychopath. Even from the written transcription of his talk, it must be clear that he lacks the cool certainty, the heedless power of his brother. Less has been written about rapists, and certainly rapists do not fit into one psychological category or any neat group of categories. Nevertheless, an article by Murray L. Cohen, Ralph Garofalo, Richard B. Boucher, and Theoharis Seghorn, "The Psychology of Rapists," identified three classes of seriously disordered rapists, one of which describes Tommy Searl with uncanny accuracy. Since this psychological pattern is not so well known, perhaps I might indicate some of the qualities that characterize rapists with "aggressive aim," the class that Tommy must belong to, if he did in fact commit the rapes.

Rapists of this group, according to Cohen and his colleagues, have the highest intelligence of any group of sexual offenders, and are usually attractive physically and attentive to health and hygiene. They are often skillful workers, usually doing "masculine" jobs like driving a truck or working in a garage. The rapes often occur in a series, and the victims are always complete strangers. Sometimes, as in Tommy's case, the rape occurs in the offender's automobile where the victim is brought by physical force or by threat with a weapon. (Otherwise, the rape occurs in the victim's home, the rapist gaining entrance by some ruse.) With this group of offenders, the sexual assault is primarily an aggressive, destructive act—not the expression of a sexual wish but an attempt to humiliate, dirty, and defile the victim. The degree of violence varies from simple assault to brutal, vicious attacks sometimes resulting in the victim's death.

The rapes usually appear as isolated episodes in an otherwise relatively normal social and psychiatric history. Many of the men are married and those who are not are engaged in dating regularly, but their relationships with women are dif-

155

ficult, marked by episodic mutual irritation and, at times, violence. They tend to see women as hostile, demanding, ungiving, and unfaithful—and frequently for good reason. The women they choose as wives and lovers are in fact assertive, active, and independent, expecting the men to accept, sometimes, a passive role that they find intolerable. Cohen and his colleagues find these rapists to be reenacting features of the Oedipal situation in their relationships with girlfriends or wives who are unfaithful or have attachments to other men. The rapes are acts of displaced rage, the result of ambivalent feelings toward the mother, or another woman who stands in for the mother.

I don't know much about Tommy Searl's relationship with his mother, but his relationship with Julie answers Cohen's description perfectly. Their marriage was fitful and violent, as we have seen, with Julie often having the upper hand. Tommy's trip to Wyoming (when his first assault on a woman occurred) was provoked by an especially intense fight with Julie. And Ralph's letters to Julie and her loyalty to him, which she acknowledged to be deeper than her attachment to Tommy, certainly created what Cohen calls an "Oedipal situation." This sexual and sibling rivalry, reenacting with complicated ferocity the normal rivalry for the mother, came to a head when Ralph was returned to Kalamazoo for retrial. Julie had recently divorced Tommy, and he knew that she was visiting Ralph in jail. This was the time when the rape-murders began.

Cohen and his colleagues observe that these rapists, afterwards, often show compassion for their victims and try to make some sort of restitution for their crimes. Their behavior in prison "is quite at odds with the primitive, brutal acts of sexual violence that brought about the commitment." This is strikingly so in Tommy's case. In addition to the gifts for the telephone operators and correspondence with children and adults in Ashford, Ohio, Tommy makes six-foot-high snowmen at Christmas time, huge snowballs, and elaborate mock fireplaces for the cell block and the visiting room.

One year his cell block got a scrawny Christmas tree, so the following year, according to Prison Counselor Walter Harmon, Tommy kept a kind of vigil at the prison delivery door so that they would be sure to get a good tree. In the prison paper and in interviews with reporters from outside prison, Tommy has supported the idea of hiring women prison guards. He thinks the inmates will be respectful and protective of them and their presence will help humanize the place. Other inmates are not necessarily pleased by his attempts to civilize the prison—sometimes after Christmas they smash his decorations—and the staff seem a little perplexed. Cohen's phrase, "make some sort of restitution," is probably as good a way as any to understand what Tommy is up to.

Though Tommy and Luke are very much alike in intelligence and talents, though they suffered through the same childhood and married the same woman, they seem to me opposite in what I might call "psychic economy." Any observer would notice it at once. A reader can sense it even in the transcriptions of their talk. Luke appears to be almost totally free of internal conflict. He can express anger, contempt, or admiration, directing his attention, with a strange purity, to people and things outside himself. If the psychologists' term *unconflicted* applies to anyone, it must apply to him. This appears to be an important source of his power, his aura, as it must be for certain politicians and businessmen. He wastes no energy on fear, regret, or uncertainty. On the other hand, watching Tommy, one is convinced, I believe, that a tremendous amount of energy is expended in internal exchanges, one part of his mind trying to prove something to another. It is as though the past has left enormous boulders in the back of his head and he now must exert great effort to ignore them, to divert our attention from them, or if possible to think them out of existence.

I found it hard to listen to him; I was tired at the end of the day. In a revealing speech, Tommy said that the conversations were tiring for him, too—and typical of the conversations he has with everyone:

I get tired of being the middle man all the time. I get tired of being the one that does all the talking. Everyone else, when I stand and listen to people talk, always seems to be bumbling around. They never say what they really want to say, they never have a solution to a problem, and they always talk things indirectly. And I can only listen to just so much of that, and I have to say something that brings things on head and on point and arrives at a solution to whatever the problem is. But I get tired of that, I get tired of being the one that's supposed to come up with ideas, that's supposed to come up with the solutions, that's supposed to come up with the good thoughts. Supposed to keep the conversation going, supposed to do this, supposed to do that.

I have a very flippant, dry sense of humor. I'll insult you in a minute, but I do it in jest, like Don Rickles or something. But people take me serious. But if I don't keep that up, I don't really know how to respond to people. If there isn't some kind of problem that has to be solved, something I have to face, I don't know how to talk to people, 'cause I can't set there and shut up. Because if I'm setting there and shutting up, most people don't talk. We just stand there staring at each other. And that makes me figure, well, what's the matter, doesn't he like me? Aren't I interesting enough or doesn't he have anything to say to me? So then I keep the chatter going and I talk and I talk and I talk and try to find an area that they're interested in. So that they can talk. And then when they get dry, I start up the conversation in some other area, but it makes me feel that I'm the one that has to drive things all the time or else everything dies. And I don't like that feeling.

I wish I could find somebody that could let me set back and listen for a while. This is the situation right here again. [The two of us talking—or, rather, him talking and me listening.] I find myself in these situations all the time. All the time, constantly. Ninety percent of my conversations are this type of a conversation: one question, twenty minutes worth of answers from me. One little comment, twenty minutes worth of conversation from me. Psychologically, it drains me. Psychologically and emotionally, it drains me. Because I seem like I'm giving and giving and giving and giving, and everybody's just taking. And I feel lost. I feel lost. I feel like I've lost in the exchange.

I'm sorry to say I did nothing to relieve the onesidedness of the conversation. I just asked another question.

Here is a man trying to keep the conversation going, to establish an exchange with other people, to "make some sort of restitution." But his speech is so driven by his own needs that his talk comes out in twenty-minute parcels. His listeners are ill at ease, and he is drained and lost.

16.

The Marijuana Bust

On November 2, 1972, Ralph Searl appeared a second time in the Kalamazoo Circuit Court, this time to plead guilty to the murder of Earl Foote. Though the plea bargain was never made public, apparently the court agreed that he be sent to the Michigan Reformatory at Ionia (rather than to Jackson or Marquette), and that his name be changed to Luke Karamazov. During the long stretches of time in the hole in Marquette, he had thought about changing his name:

> I got to know Ralph Searl. And through the gaining of that knowledge, I began to know Luke Karamazov. That was kind of a transition point. From that point on it was a constructive process. I became aware. That's probably difficult to understand, but you are what you think you are, no more, no less. I'm a firm believer in that. And at some point in those two years [in the hole], I decided I was a winner and I began to believe it. Once I began to believe it, it became true, and it was all uphill.

Karamazov's actions in Ionia reflected this change in his conception of himself. His sister says his letters became much more coherent. He married Julie and maintained a consistent concern for her and her children. Instead of being seen as a menace by prison officials, as he was in Marquette, he began to be valued as a clerk in Recreation or an assistant in Hobby Craft. The Inspector, the Director of Treatment, and the Deputy Warden respected him. He was still formidable: the dark glasses, the cool, controlled voice and eyes, the reputation for fearlessness and violence. But he was no longer tearing out earphones and demanding to be sent to the hole. By the time I met him, he was clearly one of the most influential inmates at Ionia. And he said he was happy— with his family and with his position in the institution.

I talked with Karamazov once in October, once in November, and once in December of 1976. I had arranged to see him again on February 24, 1977, but Julie called me the evening before to tell me that Luke had been busted on a marijuana charge and I wouldn't be able to visit him. Since I had an appointment with the Deputy Warden as well as Karamazov, I went up to Ionia anyway. Julie was waiting for me in the parking lot, with a message for Luke. It said that she had talked with state prison officials in Lansing and that someone was coming down from Lansing to make a thorough investigation. The note ended, "I pray I did the right thing. Please be alright." I did not get to talk with Luke, or deliver the note, but I did talk with the Deputy Warden, the Director of Treatment, and the Director of Recreation, and while walking inside the prison I saw through a glass door Luke talking with a couple of official-looking men in suits— the investigators from Lansing.

Though there were some denials at the time, the story of the bust and the investigation seems clear, at least in its outlines. Karamazov had occasionally given prison officials information, as other prisoners also did, about weapons or potential riots or hard drugs, things he now considered disruptive and likely to make the prison chaotic. Then Inspector Davis, with Glen Langdon as intermediary, asked Karamazov's help in apprehending a drug dealer inside the prison.

The understanding, more or less explicit, was that he might deal in marijuana as an entree to the larger drug operation. His cell would not be searched for a while.

But one day when Inspector Davis was off duty, the state police, possibly acting on a tip, took Karamazov to segregation, searched his cell, ripped seams in his clothes, dismantled his TV, "made a big deal search of it," as Julie said. They found marijuana. At first, Karamazov was annoyed at this apparently inadvertent violation of his understanding with the Inspector, but he was willing to wait it out. He became more than annoyed, though, as it gradually became clear that the prison officials intended to do nothing about it, to let the marijuana charge go on his record and let him serve out his time in the hole. Karamazov was outraged at what seemed to him to be treachery, flat failure to keep a bargain. He filed an appeal with the review board inside the prison. The appeal was denied.

Julie had received letters from Luke frequently during this episode, so she knew and shared his indignation, but she had not been able to talk with him directly. She went to see the Warden, and, when that did not produce results, she called Lansing and went to talk with the state prison officials. Now somebody was in trouble. It is acceptable, of course, to receive information from prisoners, but it is not proper to bargain for it. Investigators came down at once, the same day that Julie went to Lansing. The Warden and Deputy Warden denied any knowledge of the understanding with Karamazov. There was talk of lie detector tests. Then apparently Glen Langdon, who had talked so openly to me about the matter, talked with similar candor to the investigators. Further, perhaps being uneasy about what the investigators might uncover, he explained that he had accepted a watch and a purse as gifts from Karamazov.

For a while, anxiety ran fairly high among the staff, complicated by certain rivalries and antagonisms among the officials themselves. The Warden and Deputy Warden were cleared but not without turmoil. Glen Langdon was suspended and later reassigned to another prison. From Karamazov's point of view, the episode made enemies of most, or all, of the staff people he had been close to. And it was likely that the story had leaked out to other prisoners, who would have been incredulous, unable to believe that he had been a snitch—and then angry. There was talk of his life being in danger. With everyone's consent, he was transferred to the Riverside Correctional Facility, a smaller prison in the same town, one that had only recently been equipped to handle maximum security prisoners.

That is a calm and matter-of-fact summary of the marijuana bust and its consequences. But there was nothing calm or matter-of-fact about Karamazov's reaction to it. He was furious. I was surprised by the intensity of his anger and by his actions—and Julie's. As I have indicated, I had been impressed by Karamazov's self-possession. He appeared to be in perfect control of himself, his voice, his gestures, his posture, his expression (insofar as one can judge it through the dark glasses). He seemed to be thinking all the time, calculating, estimating the effects of what he was saying and doing. So I wondered about his indignation and the protest to Lansing. After all, he had worked for and achieved a privileged position at the Michigan Reformatory: the prison officials respected him, liked him in some cases, depended on him as a force for stability inside the prison, and gave him certain freedoms and privileges; lower level staff tended to be suspicious and deferential; other inmates admired him or feared him. He had a lot to lose. In taking his case to Lansing (or encouraging Julie to do so), he destroyed his relationship with the officials and jeopardized his standing among the prisoners. It seemed to me that he had lost a great deal and gained nothing. And it did not seem necessary or inevitable to me. He could have served a short term in segregation for the marijuana offense and returned to the general population with his status intact. He might even have some additional leverage with the prison officials because they would owe him something for his silence. Or that was the way the situation appeared to me.

So I asked Karamazov whether he thought it was to his advantage to bring the whole system down on himself as he did by going to Lansing. When he answered, he spoke slowly, clearly, and with great intensity.

In the first place I did not intentionally bring the system down. They are some lying son of a bitches, OK? They got their asses caught in the crack. Now they try to shift it off on me, I'm not going for it. I'm not accepting no bullshit. When they start lying on me—and they're lying all the way up to their superiors in Lansing—that's their ass. Now they're constantly telling me, don't lie, which I *don't* lie. I don't give a fuck who believes it or not, I do not lie. It's not my makeup to lie. I have never lied about killing people, I'm sure as the fuck not going to lie about some god damn marijuana. All right?

Now these little punks around here want to try to shift the weight anyway, because they're afraid to admit that they're wrong, they *used* me, that's all they did, they used me as a fucking agent, they took advantage of me, and then they want to back out and leave me hanging out in the god damn wind. I'm not going for it. Now as far as bringing the system down, *fuck* the system. I give less than a fuck what they think or what they do. They can kiss my ass—and I hope they've got this fucking room bugged so they can take it all in: Kiss my motherfucking ass.

Now as far as Langdon is concerned, he went out and told on his god damn self. He's the one who went out and told the fucking warden about the watch and the purse. I had nothing to do with it whatsoever. If anything, he fronted me off on it. Look, he can get fired and leave the fucking system. I can't. They refuse to fire me, OK, so I'm caught.

Now I'm the one who's going to pay for this little bullshit. I'm paying for it now. They're stopping Julie's mail and fucking with my mail. They're calling me out, putting pressure on me, calling Julie out putting pressure on her—to try to put more pressure on me. [To do what?] Bust other motherfuckers in here. They're trying to make everybody pay. Look, they got caught with their punk asses out, all right? The punk-ass warden lied to Lansing, based on the lies his little officials had told him and what he *wanted* to lie to them about. When they got caught in the god damn lies, he called me out and said, "I'm going to tell you right now I got you by the balls and I'm going to squeeze, cause I'm going to bust every motherfucker you ever did anything with, and you're going to pay, too." You know what he told Julie when she come up here Monday and told him she hadn't got any mail for ten days? "You're going to have to *expect* that. Luke is responsible for one of my deputies getting fired and he's gonna pay for it, he's gonna suffer for it." Now if I'm supposed to set back and accept that bullshit. . . .

At this point Karamazov broke off and said, "I don't know what that punk-ass Jespersen told you out there and I don't particularly . . ." Before I had been allowed in to see Karamazov on this visit, a guard told me that the Deputy Warden would like to speak with me. We spoke briefly in his office. He wanted to warn me that Luke could *use* his friends—and he mentioned Glen Langdon's transfer by way of example. He denied that he himself had any knowledge that Luke had marijuana in his cell. If he had known it, he probably would have gone himself and got it out of there. He had been exonerated by the Lansing investigators. He had let them know that he would fight it all the way, polygraph tests and all. He would take it to the Supreme Court if necessary. He acknowledged that they had found against Langdon for taking the watch and the wallet from Karamazov, and Inspector Davis might be in trouble, too. Jespersen asked if I could see the end of this project of mine, and I said I thought I had enough information for the time being. Now I needed to figure out what I really wanted to do with all this.

This was the context, then, when Karamazov went on to say, "I'll tell you what, you're putting a rupture between us—because you talk to that son of a bitch there. Now I know what he's after. He's after—in the first place, he's deeply concerned about what I'm gonna tell you, and he wants to know what I say. Now if you violate any of our confidence and tell him anything that I say, we're through."

In fact, I had never agreed that our conversations were confidential, except for a few, specific bits of information that he had asked me to keep off the record—mostly information about people outside of prison. But I answered more simply: "He never asked."

"Well, what is he talking to you about? What is so god damn important that he's got to see you before you see me?"

"The only thing . . . he told me he wanted to warn me against being used by you."

"Oh, OK."

"That was what he said."

"Yeah. Yeah. Do you fear that?"

"I don't see how you can use me."

"Well, what's his purpose in telling you that, then?"

"I think he may actually have thought that I might bring contraband in or something, which I haven't any . . ."

"I've never asked you to, have I?"

167

"Of course not."

"I haven't asked anyone to bring anything of any consequence in."

"He didn't make a big deal of it, he just said he wanted . . ."

"And he tried to lay that on the fact that I had somehow busted Langdon? That was the implication?"

"Well, that sometimes your friends got in trouble, I don't know, maybe that's the right way to put it."

"Trouble of their own making. I didn't twist his mother-fucking arm and put the watch on his wrist. He had a need, I offered, he accepted. He's a big boy, and he ought to pay. If he wants to go up there and tell them about it, and he gets his ass fired that's his tough luck. I could have busted his ass anywhere down the line this whole thing. I have refused absolutely to bust anybody—any of my friends—I'm not going to *do* that. They can kiss my ass."

His anger all through this talk made my initial question seem beside the point. Why had he brought the system down on himself? He didn't care about the system. They had left him hanging in the wind and he wasn't going for it. He did what he did out of indignation and outrage. Yet, during an earlier conversation, he told me that he thinks everything people do is calculated, one way or another, consciously or unconsciously. He said he is aware of how his actions or talk may affect someone else. He may tell one guard something, knowing he will tell another, who will tell a third, etc. I asked about the potato chip incident in the army—wouldn't he say that was pure impulse? No, even that may have been calculated. He was feeling under the thumb of Uncle Sam or maybe he wanted to prove his manhood to that particular group of guys. He wasn't sure how much was bluff, how much was for effect. But he didn't think of it as a burst of uncontrollable anger. The control was there, even in that incident.

So his reaction to the marijuana bust may have been controlled as well. Certainly, his manner suggested both anger and control—a kind of calm fury. If so, if he was calculating consequences as well as venting his indignation, how might the calculations have totalled up? Perhaps I was wrong in supposing that by going to Lansing and causing a furor he could only bring trouble on himself. To be sure, his relationship with the prison officials at Ionia would never be as close again. (But perhaps I am the one who values closeness; he values respect, leverage, fear.) If there was calculation along with the anger, he probably foresaw what did in fact happen: he was transferred to Riverside, a smaller and newer prison. He, the staff at the Michigan Reformatory, and the officials in Lansing all agreed that a move would be a good thing. In making that move, Karamazov gave up the hobby craft job that he had looked forward to for months, a job especially suited to his skills and one that carried a good deal of responsibility. But Riverside had great advantages. When I talked with him in August 1977, after he had been in Riverside for a few months, he reported:

> It's a lot more relaxed around here. This is the best prison I've ever been in. My room is not as big as this room [the room we were talking in, possibly nine by twelve feet], but it's damn near, damn close. I've been in cells which are half as big. I've got my own windows and screens on them I can open and close, twenty-four-hour electricity, which is unheard of in Michigan. We just don't have it anywhere else. We don't have any lavatory facilities in the cell, no sink or toilet, so consequently our doors are unlocked twenty-four hours a day. We're out until eleven o'clock and we've got a porch and we can go out and sit on the porch, kind of an air porch, you know, the air flows pretty freely. Recreation is three hours a day. You eat on the floor and the food is extraordinary, you just can't believe how good it is, I can't anyway. It's just tremendous, you know, it's a hell of a place.

169

But these ass holes will probably screw it up. Convicts, you know, they got a bad habit of screwing everything up.

Deputy Warden Jespersen predicted that after the bust and the investigation Luke wouldn't have favors from the staff for a while. But they don't have time to hold a grudge. In four months' time he'd be back in the same position. "He's competent. You count on him because you don't have anyone else to count on." This prediction proved accurate. In Riverside, Luke was made editor of the prison newspaper and Executive Secretary of the Riverside Representative Council, the organization that represents prisoners in grievances or petitions for improvement of prison conditions.

In January 1980, I talked with Charles Marshall, Corrections Officer, Counselor, and then Administrative Assistant to the Superintendent at Riverside, after Luke had been there for two and a half years. Marshall said he liked Luke. "As a resident, he doesn't make any waves. He'll come to you and say, 'Look, here's what I need.' He is always willing to help another resident—type a letter for him or show him how to research his own case, how to formulate an appeal, or who to contact. He's a good organizer. As leader of the Representative Council, he's gone about the agenda the right way. He moves among all groups in the prison and is respected by the staff." In short, Marshall talked about Karamazov in much the way James Russell and Glen Langdon had, with admiration, as though there were a personal understanding between them.

Marshall made it clear, too, that Karamazov's bearing had not changed:

Luke has an aura. You're convinced that at any moment he has the capacity to take your head off without breaking into a sweat. He doesn't get upset. He's so assured, you think he must know what he is doing. When you come to a reformatory—any prison—you've got to establish your territory *right now.* Luke can lay that cold look on you and you'd better back up. He has a certain amount of territory within the Department of Corrections and you don't come within that territory.

Marshall didn't say that Karamazov had a certain amount of territory within the prison, he said within the Department of Corrections. Presumably he meant that other prisoners kept their distance, treated him with respect (or fear) but also that the staff did as well—and not just the staff at Riverside but the staff within the state prison system. If that is true, as I believe it is, then his fury over the marijuana bust takes on a different color. By encouraging Julie to go to Lansing and bringing down on himself the wrath of those who seemed to be his friends, he was also staking out territory for himself. He was serving notice to the Ionia staff that he understood the prison system as well as they did. He knew when they had acted improperly and, if pushed, he knew how to make the most of their vulnerability. Even though he was the prisoner and they were his keepers, still he might have power over them. In going to Lansing, he was not, as I first thought, recklessly jeopardizing his favored position within the prison. His position was not so fragile. It depended less on good will than on competence and control. While he was acting out of real anger at the injustice that he believed had been done him, he was at the same time asserting power and preparing for a move to a smaller, more comfortable prison. Impulse and calculation coincided neatly.

17.

Images of Control

Early in January 1980, I sent Luke Karamazov a draft of the first hundred pages or so of the manuscript of this book, and on January 18 my colleague Robert Grossman and I drove to Ionia to talk with him. Grossman is a clinical psychologist, a direct, shrewd, impressive person, who had worked for a number of years at the Kalamazoo Regional Psychiatric Hospital before coming to Kalamazoo College. He had heard me talk about Karamazov and had listened to tapes of some of his conversations. He was interested in meeting him in person. And Karamazov liked the idea of meeting a psychologist who had been thinking about him at a distance. Earlier, when I wrote that I might bring Grossman along, he replied in a letter to me:

> And yes, I would like to meet your friend Bob—do please feel free to bring him along—I hope he won't be reticent about his observations concerning the Karamazov!? You MUST have guessed that I couldn't possibly resist meeting and speaking to some one who has "viewed" me, and especially one such who has been trained in the mental arts!? My wandering, wondering whimsical

narcissism demands such a meeting. Hummm, I was being epigrammatic in that last thought, but there are always grains of truth in all humor, aren't there?

On the way to Ionia, Grossman asked me how I thought Karamazov would react to the manuscript. I wasn't sure. He had certainly been friendly and relaxed in his letter, before he received the manuscript. I knew he might be annoyed by some of my comments, but I thought he would be pleased to see how much space I had given to the transcription of his own words. He is a good talker, and I had given him room to tell his own story. I thought he would be satisfied—even flattered.

I was wrong. The first thing he said to me, when we were led into the small prison conference room, was, "I am very displeased with you. . . . I can't possibly conceive of what you think you're doing. In the first place, you're jeopardizing my life with confidential information, OK? That's the paramount thing. Were you aware of that?" He was thinking of the chapter "Friends in Ionia" in which I talk about his collaboration with prison officials, something not likely to make a prisoner popular with other inmates. I felt I was on solid ground. None of the information was confidential: he and the prison officials had talked freely with me, knowing that I intended to write something. No one had indicated that any of the information was off the record. Furthermore, I couldn't believe that he was in real danger. Almost three years had passed since the marijuana bust, and nothing had happened, even though he told me, at the time, that word of his collaboration had probably leaked out to other inmates. Riverside Prison, whose population is made up largely of special groups—juvenile offenders, psychiatric and geriatric cases, prisoners who are there for protection, etc.—is not as dangerous as Jackson, Marquette, or the Reformatory at Ionia, and it seemed clear that Karamazov was one of its most powerful and respected residents. So I didn't

believe that his life was in danger or that my reporting was
improper. Still, I was taken aback by the force of his charge. I
had seen the intensity of his anger before, but this was the
first time I had seen it directed at me.

Karamazov wanted to know what I was attempting to
prove in this book. He opened the manuscript and quoted a
few sentences:

> Following our first meeting, my central impression
> was one I have not adequately conveyed yet, but
> one that will become clear as we go on—an impres-
> sion of intensity and power. Certainly he was affa-
> ble and courteous, making the visit much easier
> than I had imagined it might be. At the same time,
> he seemed completely in control, saying just what
> he intended to say, well aware of the impressions
> he was conveying. He might well be a genius at
> improvising, I thought, and his improvisations
> probably included manipulation of people as
> well . . .

That passage seemed to him outrageous:

> Damn. God. Where? Why? You're describing here
> a person that I would think was quite well adjusted
> to life in a very difficult situation, and then you
> twist it around and make me into some kind of a
> Machiavellian manipulator. Why? What are you
> intending to prove with stuff like that? Don't you
> see what you're doing? You meet a person who's
> in control of himself, who hasn't allowed this shit
> system that we've got to fuck his head up, who
> stays on top of things and tries to be of value to this
> community, and then you make me out to be some
> kind of ogre or something.

I said I was surprised the passage came across as negatively
as it seemed to. But he insisted, "It's there. What possible
interpretation . . ." I interrupted to ask if he was not aware

of his own power. He said, "Certainly. Do *you* have power? Do you have power in your classroom, do you control and manipulate that class and shape it?" I agreed that I do. "Does that make you an ogre?" I said I hadn't called him an ogre. "Well, that's what you're calling me at base here. You're saying this is a sinister thing because this person is in control of himself."

Karamazov asked Bob Grossman how *he* interpreted that passage. Grossman said he saw the person described there as being very sensitively aware of his environment and very competent within the framework of that environment, someone who was intellectually sophisticated and sharp. But Karamazov was not going to be diverted by praise. "Do you know what *manipulative* means in here?" Maybe I don't, I admitted. "It's the worst crime in prison. The very worst." OK, what does it mean? "It means that you are manipulative, that you control your environment. That's the worst possible thing you can do in prison. That's the dirtiest word in this whole vocabulary in prison." We talked some more, agreeing that he *did* control his environment, but we did not arrive at an acceptable way to talk about that control.

In the manuscript, I mentioned the "casually remorseless way" Karamazov spoke of the murder of five men. He objected to that phrase; this apparent remorselessness deserved a closer look. First, he reminded me that he had turned himself in after the murders, believing that Michigan still had capital punishment. And after the knife incident in the army, he turned himself in, "because I'd had it up to here with doing what I was doing for that hour or so." Similarly, in the case of the murders, "you look back on yourself and say, what am I doing? Stop this. I think it suggests something other than remorselessness."

Second, when it comes to telling about the murders, "I've said these things for years and years and years and years. A lot of people are always asking, and I have a policy of not being dishonest about it. So I've said it thousands of times and it's become an old story. . . . What did you do?

How did you do it? And it ends up being thousands of times over the years that I've told that story, so there's that callousness of repetition that overlays the whole thing. I can tell the story by rote and I don't have to think about it when I'm telling it."

Third, though the killings themselves were unemotional, even mechanical, and the account of the murders has become overlaid with the callousness of repetition, there was a time in between, Karamazov said, when he felt for the victims. "I suppose the enormity of the whole thing struck me in court, the first time I saw his [Foote's] wife and kids, two little kids if I remember right, and that just freaked me out. The only thing that ever bothered me in court was that. Suddenly they're two little kids that don't have a father anymore, and it just brought it all home."

Finally, he brought the argument back to the project of this book:

> You know it comes back to, Conrad, what the fuck do I *do* with it? All right? Do I set down and cry all day long every day or do I attempt to do something constructive? That's what I intend to do. I intend to do something constructive for this community, for myself, and for other people who are close to me. This whole undertaking here [the book] is something that I consider to be a constructive undertaking. When we first talked—I don't want to talk about money, I'm not even considering it, I don't even look for any. All I'm looking for is an objective, nonsensational treatment of me, because hopefully there might be someone that has the same symptoms, they might be able to see it and stop it. It's a forlorn hope probably but a hope nonetheless.

Much of the tension had gone out of the air by now—though immediately following the speech above, Karamazov said, "I guess I hoped for something different. Truth of the matter was I just put a lot of faith in you, a lot of trust, and I didn't consider what you *could* do." Bob Grossman asked Karamazov what he thought the differences were between himself (Karamazov) and me. "Day and night," he said. He went on to say that he could picture Grossman and himself talking in the prison yard if they were in prison together. He couldn't put me in that picture. I wouldn't fit.

I asked if there were spots in the manuscript where I had misunderstood something he said, and he did point out some specific slips of that kind. For example, I had thought he was picked up in Mexico by the Mexican police, whereas in fact it was the Texas Rangers who picked him up. And I had not been clear about the pistols—that he had traded the Ruger Bearcat for the double-barrelled Derringer. Before we left, he said he thought a lot of the problems would be resolved if I used fictitious names. I made no promises then, but later I decided he was right. We parted on fairly friendly terms.

Looking back on it, I think the subject of that last meeting was control—self-control, control of other people, and control of the manuscript. Now, having let him have his say, perhaps I can end the book with some consideration of control itself. Karamazov seems to me preoccupied with control; perhaps he has to be to clear space for himself in prison and within the Department of Corrections. And I, if I see myself clearly, am not much interested in exercising control and not much good at it—except when I am in front of a typewriter or a class. I sometimes wish I were more adept at managing power, kneading the world into a more agreeable shape, but mainly I hope for the opposite: I would like to learn what every comic artist is trying to teach me—to be negligent of self, to be foolish, to let go.

But this book is about Karamazov, not me. Thinking back over his talk, his life as he remembers it, I am struck by how many images there are of control and power—or their counterpart, images of frustrating powerlessness: shooting bank swallows, fighting for a quarter on the rug, refusing to be put down by a science teacher, extorting milk money from school kids, fighting with Tommy for Julie or Martha Gillman, flourishing knives in the army, taking gas station attendants to the back room and shooting them, locking Foote in the trunk of his car and shooting him when he refused to do what he was told, talking to a policeman at the roadblock, constructing the spider and fly machine, reforming conditions in the hole at Marquette, knowing how to open doors at Ionia, sending Julie to Lansing to protest an injustice.

And how few images there are of discovery, luck, or receptivity. The ride with Mike and the chimpanzee has more of a tone of openness and adventure than the other stories he told me. The very fact that his gun was gone, that he was dependent on Mike's whim or calculation, gives that episode an element of surprise, gaiety almost, that seems quite absent from the other stories. But even there, Karamazov and Mike were jockeying for control, and part of Karamazov's pleasure must have come from the discovery that he could exercise control even without a gun. In all that Karamazov told me, I can remember only one picture that is completely free of the drive for power or control. It is the picture of himself sitting in front of the basement fireplace in Ben Barrett's house on the farm—just sitting and watching the flames. That single image makes clear how purposeful all the other stories are, with what a tight hand Karamazov holds on to events.

I have mentioned Ernest Becker from time to time. I would like to return to him now for a somewhat more formal discussion of the kind of control Karamazov exercises, and its limitations. To recapitulate Becker's observation, human beings are caught in a unique and unavoidable dilemma: on one hand, we have astounding powers of perception, memory, analysis, imagination—and we know it. We each feel our own uniqueness and grandeur; we should be gods. But we can't help noticing that our remarkable powers are attached to a dying animal. In order to live our lives, we must to some extent repress our awareness of death, or we would constantly be overwhelmed by the sense of absurdity and terror. This repression takes any number of forms, but we may reduce them to two. The first we have already seen, blatantly, in Ralph Searl: the drive for heroism, for cosmic recognition, even if it means suicide or murder. The second form we have mentioned only in passing: the reduction of the universe to a manageable size. If one thinks in small enough terms—my neighborhood, my school, my company—it is almost possible to believe that one can control events. The rackety force of irrational time and accident can be pushed far to the back of the mind. If we concentrate hard enough on ourselves and our immediate surroundings, we can forget about death for months or years at a time.

Becker, paraphrasing Kierkegaard, uses the metaphor of a prison for the supposedly safe world people draw in around themselves:

> Like many prisoners, they are comfortable in their limited and protected routines, and the idea of a parole into the wide world of chance, accident, and choice terrifies them. . . . In the prison of one's character one can pretend and feel that he *is somebody*, that the world is manageable, that there is a reason for one's life, a ready justification for one's action. To live automatically and uncritically is to be assured of at least a minimum share of the programmed cultural heroics—what we might call "prison heroism": the smugness of the insiders who "know." (Becker, 86–87)

In the case of Luke Karamazov, of course, it is no metaphor. His universe has shrunk to a literal prison which he can understand and manage with considerable precision and subtlety. Up to the time of his arrest, he may be seen as the classic case of a psyche calling out for recognition, impulsively and recklessly insisting on heroism, demanding a last supper. After his arrest (though the transition was gradual), he becomes the paradigm of the controller, tempering impulse with calculation and becoming a specialist in the management of power in a closed system. Karamazov exemplifies with unambiguous clarity the two devices that are available to disguise our real standing in the universe: making ourselves larger than we are and making the world smaller. And he seems to have succeeded as few people can. I detect very little doubt, nothing that could be called fear and trembling, in his manner. (Tommy, by contrast, seems to me to be living on the rim of emptiness, as though in an inattentive moment a small push could send him over.)

Up to this point, I have oversimplified Becker's argument. He finds in humans not just the desire to assert their own individuality, their own permanent specialness, but also an opposite urge to become part of what is vastly greater than they are.

> Here we have to introduce a paradox that seems to go right to the heart of organismic life and that is especially sharpened in man. The paradox takes the form of two motives or urges that seem to be part of creature consciousness and that point in two opposite directions. On the one hand the creature is impelled by a powerful desire to identify with the cosmic process, to merge himself with the rest of nature. On the other hand he wants to be unique, to stand out as something different and apart. (Becker, 151–52)

Becker believes that these conflicting pulls make it impossible for most humans to feel "right" in any straightforward way. Most of us feel strongly the attraction that he calls Agape, the desire to merge ourselves with something grander and less vulnerable. Rank speaks of our yearning for "a feeling of kinship with the All." This impulse must be central to all religious experience and to much art. At the same time, most of us feel the impulse that Becker calls Eros, the drive

181

toward individual heroism, the desire for personal power and control, the impulse to "stick out of nature and shine." (Becker, 153)

> Now we see what we might call the ontological or creature tragedy that is so peculiar to man: If he gives in to Agape he risks failing to develop himself, his active contribution to the rest of life. If he expands Eros too much he risks cutting himself off from natural dependency, from duty to a larger creation; he pulls away from the healing power of gratitude and humility that he must naturally feel for having been created, for having been given the opportunity of life experience. (Becker, 153)

Thus Becker offers one way of talking about Luke Karamazov's limitations and the source of his intensity and power. Karamazov feels with full force the demands of Eros, the urge for the development of his own powers, his "genius." But just as his attachment to other people seems tenuous, so I venture to say his feeling of creatureliness, Agape, his attachment to the universe, is thin. He has spoken of himself as a lone wolf. Gratitude and humility seem to have little hold on him. His story is full of images of control, with almost no images of reception or wonder or letting-go. Without this counter-pull, this built-in reminder of human dependence and insignificance, it may be easier for Karamazov than for most of us to raise himself to heroic stature and shrink the world until it is only a little larger than the prison.

If this is true, we might wonder how Karamazov would feel about getting out of prison, if that should ever be possible. (In Michigan, a first-degree murder conviction carries a mandatory life sentence, without possibility of parole. But eventually these convictions are sometimes commuted by the Governor to second-degree murder so that the prisoners may be paroled.) Probably he himself does not know, for sure, how he would feel about it. Occasionally, he spoke of

things he would like to do if he were out. In our last interview, for example, he spoke of running some sort of home
for juvenile offenders: "My plan, if I ever get out of this
place, is to provide an environment for juveniles who are on
the road to this, hopefully to change their minds through
some of the things I've learned. . . . I know it wouldn't be
easy. It wouldn't be easy at all. It would be a very difficult
job, a twenty-four-hour-a-day job. But it's much more enjoyable to work for the survival of someone else than just me."

But on other occasions, he said he liked it in prison, he
enjoyed every day. When I saw him in Riverside, in 1977, I
asked directly how he would feel about being released:

> I was talking to a counselor just before I came down
> and he was saying, "What do you look for in life, do
> you want to get out of here?" No, not particularly,
> it's not important because there's too many ques-
> tions, too many fears. I don't know if I got out of
> here today, what about next week, what if, God
> forbid, Julie and I broke up or something next week,
> there was some insurmountable problem that we
> just couldn't deal with. What then? Where do I go
> from there? I'm afraid I'd go back there, and it
> doesn't seem very desirable. [Shooting people
> again? I ask.] Yes. I mean I could get into being a
> vengeance killer. There's a lot of people I would
> love to kill, because they've done me wrong or—I'd
> love to kill Tom, I would love to. I would thoroughly
> enjoy it. I mean I think he deserves dying.
>
> But it's different. You know when you drift
> and you're blowing with the wind for so long and
> then you find a degree of stability and a purpose in
> life—right now life is good for me, I thoroughly
> enjoy every day. But I don't consider where I've
> been and I don't consider where I'm going. I'm
> compartmentized into this particular time and

place and I enjoy it. It would be a hell of a transition to contemplate going to another state of being, like a free state or an alone state. I don't want to contemplate them now.

"Drifting" and "blowing with the wind" may not describe very accurately the fierce clawing for recognition and control that characterized Karmazov's life from childhood until the time of the murders. But the rest of this statement seems to me articulate and clearheaded. He can imagine vividly enough the threatening shapelessness of a larger world, the dangers that might lie outside, in his relationship with Julie or in an impulse to take revenge. He willingly chooses the stability of a life he knows, where borders are defined and behavior can be predicted. Without considering where he has been or where he is going, he accepts the compartment of a particular time and place and enjoys it.

When I first read about the Searl brothers or spoke with them, my impulse was to recoil from the cruelty and violence of their past. Now I suppose my reaction has been tempered by the "callousness of repetition" that Karamazov spoke of. I have got used to their grisly stories from retelling them myself. But the texture of their lives, the movement of their speech and thought, is still arresting. They seem to be unusually vivid examples of well-defined psychological types. More than that, the Searls help to illuminate some larger patterns: we may see them as extreme instances of behavior and states of mind that all of us share. We all sometimes replay the past, remaking pieces of our lives as we wish they had been; Tommy Searl, I believe, takes this on as the main project of his life—wrestling with the past in his own mind, making restitution, demonstrating to himself and everyone else that he could not have been the person who committed the ugly rapes and murders. Afraid of self-discovery, he seems to be walking the very edge of meaninglessness.

At the opposite extreme, Luke Karamazov exaggerates our moments of single-minded aim and action. He expresses anger, contempt, or pleasure with uncomplicated frankness; he acts, directing his energy outside himself with a pure intensity. We who doubt ourselves may te tempted to envy him—until we notice what he and Tommy both lack: the pull that Becker calls Agape, the urge to link ourselves with something whose scale is entirely beyond us.

Speaking of his murders, Karamazov said, "There has to be some part of me left out." In order to get a full sense of what is left out, we must go outside the story of the Searl brothers, to religion, literature, or myth. What is left out is the impulse to find one's life by losing it. It is Hamlet's realization, after the trip to England, that he cannot control events, that "the readiness is all." It is the receptivity one finds all through William Stafford's poetry, the responsiveness to wind, empty space, and the small gestures of the prairie. One of the simplest expressions of this impulse is found in a letter written by William Carlos Williams. He speaks of something that happened when he was about twenty, "a sudden resignation to existence, a despair—if you wish to call it that, but a despair which made everything a unit and at the same time a part of myself. I suppose it might be called a sort of nameless religious experience. I resigned, I gave up." (*Selected Letters*, 147). Out of that giving up came his poems.

In spite of Karamazov's intimate acquaintance with the fact of death, the world seems to cause him little anxiety. Extending himself to heroic proportions and shrinking the world to a prison system which can be understood and, within limits, controlled, he has escaped the uncertainty that haunts most people, the awareness of their own absurd fragility. But in escaping that, he is missing, too, the sense of creatureliness, the exhilaration of giving up or letting go, the momentary sense of kinship with a universe whose truly reckless grandeur dwarfs all human heroics.

Appendix

Summaries of the traits associated with antisocial personalities are often oddly contradictory, as in one widely used textbook: "Typically intelligent, spontaneous, and very likable on first acquaintance, anti-social personalities are deceitful and manipulative, callously using others to achieve their own ends. Often they seem to live in a series of present moments, without consideration for the past or future" (James C. Coleman, James N. Butcher, and Robert C. Carson, *Abnormal Psychology and Modern Life* [New York, 1980], 284). One might ask how they can be manipulative, using others for their own ends, if they live only in the present without consideration for the future. Theodore Millon has called attention to this contradiction: "Some clinicians have described [psychopaths] as impulsive, immature, naive, aimless and flighty. No less frequently it has been said that they are sly, cunning, and well-educated sorts who are capable of making clever long-range plans to deceive and exploit others." (Theodore Millon, *Disorders of Personality DSM-III: Axis II* [New York, 1981], 204). Millon explains this confusion by observing that "antisocial behaviors may spring from appreciably different personality combinations or mixtures." Not all antisocial personalities are alike, he suggests; some may be impulsive, others cleverly foresighted. The account of Karamazov's behavior in a preceding chapter ("The Marijuana Bust") may introduce another possibility: in some cases they may be impulsive and calculating at the same time.

The trait that would seem to distinguish Karamazov most sharply from the textbook antisocial personality, companionless or capable of only shallow or fleeting loyalties, is his attachment first to Betty Fitzell and then to Julie. Those attachments were genuine, I'm sure, and they *do* separate Karamazov from the classic psychopath. Nevertheless, in a letter dated November 7, 1979, he writes, at the end of a paragraph, "I might add that there is no longer a Julie and children in my life." In my reply, I asked about this new development. He wrote (on November 29):

> Hello, received your note. The why's and wherefore's of no more wife and kids is very much the mystery to me that it is to you! I really wasn't privy to *all* of the reasoning between her departure—just a few scattered tid bits of information here and there. Doubtless this is a subject that could best be conveyed verbally, so I'll consider sharing it in December if/when you can make it up. . . . Be sure to request that this be a noncounting visit—my likely next wife will be coming in from Colorado at Xmas and all visits are promised to her.

I didn't inquire into the details of Julie's leaving, since that seemed to me beyond the scope of the book, but Luke said that the difficulty lay in the situation, his being in prison, rather than in the relationship between himself and Julie. He was married again in May of 1980.

Works Cited

Becker, Ernest. *The Denial of Death*. New York: The Free Press, 1975.

Cleckley, Hervey. *The Mask of Sanity*. 5th ed. St. Louis: Mosby, 1976.

Cohen, Murray L., Ralph Garofalo, Richard B. Boucher, and Theoharis Seghorn. "The Psychology of Rapists." In *Forcible Rape*, edited by Duncan Chappell, Robley Geis, and Gilbert Geis, 291–314. New York: Columbia University Press, 1977.

Coleman, James C., James N. Butcher, Robert C. Carson. *Abnormal Psychology and Modern Life*. New York: Scott Foresman, 1980.

McCord, William and Joan. *The Psychopath*. Princeton: Van Nostrand, 1964.

Millon, Theodore. *Disorders of Personality DSM-III: Axis II*. New York: Wiley, 1981.

Williams, William Carlos. *Selected Letters*. New York: McDowell, Obolensky, 1957.

Conrad Hilberry is professor of English at Kalamazoo College. He received his B.A. from Oberlin College and his Ph.D. from the University of Wisconsin. As a poet he has won fellowships from the National Endowment for the Arts, and the 1984 artists award from the Michigan Foundation for the Arts. His latest book of poems, **The Moon Seen as a Slice of Pineapple**, was published in 1984 by the University of Georgia Press. He is one of the editors of **The Third Coast**, an anthology of Michigan poetry, published in 1976 by the Wayne State University Press.

The manuscript was prepared for publication by Irene Bintz. The book was designed by Don Ross. The typeface for the text is Palatino. The typefaces for the display are Stencil and Helvetica.

Manufactured in the United States of America.